NO STRANGERS TO VIOLENCE
NO STRANGERS TO LOVE

M

Twentieth Century Christian Heroes:

NO STRANGERS TO VIOLENCE
NO STRANGERS TO LOVE

Boniface Hanley, O.F.M.

AVE MARIA PRESS   Notre Dame, Indiana 46556

Imprimi Potest:
Alban A. Maguire, O.F.M.
Minister Provincial

Contents

Author's Foreword

I remember when I was a little boy, asking my mother, "Ma, what's it like to live through a war?" "I hope," she replied, "you never find out." Like everyone who shared this planet during the 20th century, I found out.

Ours has been a murderous century. Together we have written the most tragic chapter in the history of our poor battered race. Yet in the darkness, there are stars—men and women of faith and courage. For the most part, they are tiny stars. Sometimes clouds obscured them. Sometimes they flickered and almost went out. But somehow they gained new strength, new courage and new life. They refused to go out.

These people, whose stories I so briefly relate in this modest little book, were no strangers to our century's rampant violence. War, revolution, suicide or genocide trapped them as it did so many of us. The Nazis and communists killed five of them. One wore out his life in the jungles of Southeast Asia. Another died in China during the communist revolution. A nervous teenager assassinated one; another saw her father fatally shoot her mother and then kill himself. Each of them refused to despair. Instead, these bitter realities became for every one of them the occasion for profound human growth.

In the midst of the terror, they found God. Finding God they came to love themselves and to forgive and even love their persecutors and murderers. Their stories become for us a source of hope and joy.

In the third century, the writer Tertullian, sore at heart at the butchery his fellow Christians were suffering in pagan Rome prophesied: "The blood of martyrs is the seed of Christians." The following century, Christians came up from the catacombs, spread throughout Europe and shaped the course of Western Civilization. In our violent century, hundreds of thousands of Christians endured death rather than abandon their faith. We believe the blood they shed is indeed the seed of a new Christian era.

Thomas Dooley

"Now Pat, don't you worry. I'll be OK. They've made fantastic gains with cancer research." The speaker was a 33-year-old American doctor, and he was slowly dying. His name—Thomas Anthony Dooley.

Dooley was with Patricia Christensen McCarthy, riding in a small airplane high above Cambodia in February 1960. The two were using the flight time to check proofs of a book he was preparing for publication. As they worked, Dooley continued his cheerful and confident chatter. "I'll be good as new in a short time—just wait and see, Pat," he assured her.

He had almost convinced Patricia that indeed there was nothing to worry about when something in the proofs caught his attention. Dooley bent over the page, made a correction, and then, sitting up straight, stared out the plane's tiny window. It was then Patricia McCarthy realized that though Dr. Dooley's Irish tongue could weave a spell, the Irish eyes that gave his face its intensity and gentleness could not lie. More than any words, they reflected the pain that ravaged his body and the bewilderment afflicting his strong spirit.

"I had a hard time," Patricia later remembered, "holding back my tears."

11

Patricia must have remembered many things as the small aircraft flew through the clear blue skies and white puffy clouds that afternoon. She must have recalled her first meeting with him when Dooley was a freshman at the University of Notre Dame. It was the fall of 1943, and Dooley, 16, had just entered the university. He was tall, slender, curly-haired, blue-eyed, and full of fun. "His eyelashes," Pat recalled, "were devastating."

During that fall Pat invited him to Sunday afternoon parties at her home in LaPorte, Indiana. If during these gatherings Dooley won the young women's admiration, he also earned their boyfriends' envy when the girls abandoned them to crowd around the piano Dooley so skillfully played. The young men suffered even further when Dooley began to jitterbug with the delighted girls. He could, without missing a step, gracefully flip his partner over his back as he danced. "It was something," Pat wrote, "that we hadn't seen outside the movies."

Tom Dooley spent many Sundays in LaPorte, but it was not long before the hot winds of war swept over these young people. Within months some were in combat, others wounded, others dead. The young girls would mature, perhaps too soon, as the young men, one by one, went off to the battles. Because he was only 16, Dooley had nearly a year and a half before he would be eligible for the military draft. But even in those days, he was a man in a hurry, and in 1944, after he had completed three semesters in Notre Dame's accelerated wartime program, he enlisted in the United States Navy as a medic. Aside from his impulsiveness, Tom felt a serious responsibility toward his country. His older half-brother, Earle, whom Tom adored, was an infantry officer in France. After participating in the great invasion of Europe in June, Earle sustained wounds at St. Lo. As soon as he was released from the hospital, he rejoined his division, was wounded again, and returned to combat a third time. In November 1944, during the battle of Hurtgen Forest, Earle Dooley was killed.

The young lieutenant had prepared a letter to be sent home in the event of his death.

> My leaving you is important to you, I know. But in the overall picture it is not so important. . . . What is important, and I charge each of you to keep this in mind, is that this war shall never happen again. . . . You must see to it that any at-

tempt to begin this slaughter anew is crushed at once. . . .
Never again must you allow human stupidity to look idly
aside while this scourge is permitted to fester and spring out
on such a scale.

Those words of Tom's fallen hero began the slow and mysterious process of transforming the dashing young Tom Dooley into a man of great vision and profound compassion.

The change was slow and barely perceptible at first. Its foundation had already been established, of course, during the first years of Tom Dooley's childhood and early youth.

*   *   *   *   *

Tom was born into a comfortable middle-class family in St. Louis, Missouri. His father, Thomas Dooley II, had been a major of engineers in World War I. At the time of Tom's birth, January 17, 1927, Mr. Dooley was an officer in the American Car and Foundry Co., in St. Louis. Agnes Wise, Tom's mother, was a descendant of a Pennsylvania banking family. She had been married previously to an American flight officer who had been killed in an air crash at Hickam Field, Hawaii. Young Earle who had died in France was Agnes' son by her first marriage.

By 1931 the Dooley family numbered four sons: Earle, Tom, Malcolm and Edward. A close family, the Dooleys enjoyed their summer

"The villagers who come to our clinic are wonderful people," Dooley wrote after establishing his first dispensary in Laos.

vacations in Wisconsin when their father could devote full time to them. Although he was a firm disciplinarian, the boys nevertheless adored Thomas Dooley II. He was the boss in the Dooley family, and no one dared question it. More than one of his qualities rubbed off on young Thomas.

After Tom graduated from high school, he enrolled at the University of Notre Dame as a premedical student. Mr. Dooley had serious misgivings about the decision. He thought his son lacked the patience a good physician needs. He was willing, however, to give Tom the opportunity to find out for himself.

After only a year and a half at Notre Dame, Tom entered the Navy. Soon after his enlistment Tom was sent to the U.S. Navy Hospital at St. Albans in Long Island. As a medic he saw firsthand what Earle had described as "the scourge of war." Day by day young Dooley cared for boys, very often still in their teens, who had suffered severe war wounds. Some would die and others survive as cripples for life. Tom, however, was not one to wring his hands in dismay. He worked as hard as he could, and his cheerful disposition soon made him a great favorite among the patients. Even at this age he used his incomparable gift of words to encourage and cheer the wounded crammed into St. Albans' long wards.

On one of his liberty days he traveled to New York to see Hildegarde, the lovely popular singer. Tom thoroughly enjoyed Hildegarde's act and afterward went to her dressing room, knocked on the door, and barged in. He advised the astounded performer of the great popularity she enjoyed with the sick and wounded sailors at St. Albans. "When I told them this afternoon that I was going to see you, they all cried out and shouted, 'Tom, bring her back to see us. We want Hildegarde!' You simply must come and visit them," the sailor commanded.

Although a show-business veteran, Hildegarde could not withstand the Dooley avalanche of words and charm. The very next day she came, unannounced, to the hospital at St. Albans and demanded to see young sailor Dooley. With his superior officers trailing behind him, Dooley ushered Hildegarde from ward to ward where she sang for the delighted sailors.

After the war Tom returned to his premedical studies at Notre Dame and at the Sorbonne in France. In the spring of 1948 he entered medical school at St. Louis University. Just two months after Tom entered the university, his father died.

It turned out that Mr. Dooley's misgivings about Tom's suitability for a medical career were not unfounded. Tom found medical school so boring that he frequently skipped class. He wasn't wasting his time, but he preferred to engage in more practical aspects of medical activity. Some faculty members complained to the dean, Dr. Melvin Casberg, about Dooley's unorthodox approach to his medical training. Fortunately for Dooley, the dean was a perceptive man. "I recognized a heart," Dr. Casberg later recalled, "which could not be restrained within the boundaries of the routine things of life."

Somehow Dooley survived faculty displeasure, his own restlessness, and boredom of school to earn his medical degree in March 1953.

A month later Tom rejoined the United States Navy and was commissioned a lieutenant junior grade. After a little over a year at naval hospitals in Camp Pendleton, California, and in Japan, the Navy assigned him as medical officer aboard the attack transport *USS Montague*. Tom didn't know it when he boarded the ship, but he was about to begin his voyage into destiny.

$$*\quad *\quad *\quad *\quad *$$

In August 1954 the *USS Montague* was ordered to take station in the Gulf of Tonkin, off Haiphong, Vietnam. The ship was to participate in an operation called Passage to Freedom. Like most Americans, Dooley had barely heard of Indochina and Vietnam and had no real understanding of the nature of the struggle rending that unhappy country. The *Montague*'s crew knew their mission was connected with the movement of refugees—and little else.

The convulsion then gripping Vietnam was but one stage in the tragedy that country was destined to suffer. The struggle between the Vietnamese and French colonial rulers, which had been going on for a long time, took a nasty turn during and after World War II. Under Ho Chi Minh the Vietnamese rebels had defeated the French forces at Dien Bien Phu in 1954 and forced the French to sue for peace. The Treaty of Geneva, which established the peace, divided Vietnam into two zones of political influence: the North, under Communist control, and the South. The treaty gave the Vietnamese people a year to choose which half of their now-divided country they wished to inhabit. This provision of the treaty provoked one of the greatest migrations in Southeast Asian history. Hundreds of thousands of Vietnamese left the northern portion of the country to journey to the South. They left behind their homes, their lands and, in some cases, their parents. They took with them only what they could carry on their backs. This human tide funneled down from the northern provinces to Haiphong, the seaport town of Hanoi. The first trickle of refugees had already made its way to Haiphong when the *Montague* arrived. Dooley's fluency in French proved invaluable as the ship joined three other U.S. naval vessels sent by the government in August 1954 to assist the French in moving the huge throng of escapees by ship to Saigon in the South. For Dooley and his shipmates, the sea journeys were an experience they would never forget.

*   *   *   *   *

Exhausted, sick and full of fear, refugees stumbled into camps as they fled North Vietnam. For many it was a bitter Way of the Cross.

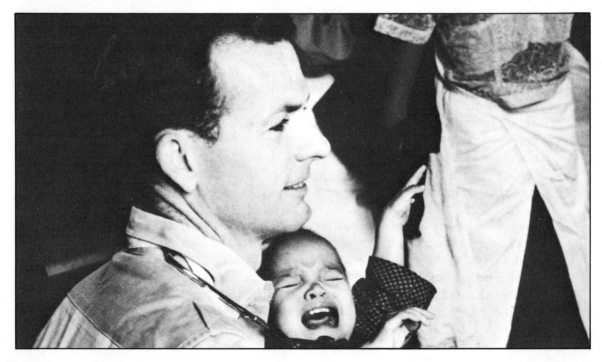

"Dooley," Commander Amberson of the Medical Corps was speaking, "your job will be to build refugee camps—as many as are needed. Now get going and don't bother me about details. . . ."

"Details," the 27-year-old doctor groaned. "I don't know the difference between a refugee camp and a playground for girls." But Dr. Dooley soon learned. He walked through the mud flats and rice paddies of Haiphong and found refugees squatting in miserable knots everywhere. These first groups from the North were a woeful lot. Frightened and bewildered, these poor wanderers were afflicted with a whole catalog of diseases. Dooley's practiced eye quickly spotted yaws, the symptoms of tuberculosis, the trachoma and swollen livers of underfed children. With the help of the French military and anybody else he could dragoon, Dr. Dooley soon had his first refugee camp established on the flats of Haiphong. He set up a tent city capable of handling 12,000 refugees at a time. He called this first of his camps, his favorite, Camp de la Pagode.

Where did he get such a name? "The name seemed Oriental and mellifluous, despite the fact the area was fresh out of pagodas," Dooley later wrote. At Camp de la Pagode, Dooley established the routine he would follow during his year at this camp and later at the other camps he would build. After assisting at daily Mass, he held sick call. This would keep him busy for most of the day. "I saw in the space of my first year a range of diseases," the doctor claimed, "that most physicians wouldn't see in a lifetime." He had to treat these diseases before the Navy crammed the refugees on the ships to take them south.

In October the Navy transferred Amberson and appointed Dooley commanding officer. To help him in his enormous task, Dr. Dooley organized a small staff of Navy medics. These men dedicated themselves, without reserve, to the work. So successful was Dooley and indeed the entire naval force engaged in the operation, that they moved more than 600,000 people without a serious epidemic breaking out.

Dooley's concern spread far beyond the medical needs of the refugees. He studied thoroughly the origins of the Vietnam conflict and tried to understand the reasons that drove these people to make the enormous sacrifice of leaving everything behind to face an uncertain future in the South. Dooley's superior officers encouraged him to share his knowledge with the men participating in the operation, Passage to Freedom. The young doctor prepared a series of lectures and delivered them to the officers and men of the naval squadron on station off Haiphong. Dooley felt that if the men understood the origins of the war, they could appreciate the heroism and love of liberty these miserable-looking refugees whom they were hauling down the South China Sea possessed. And Dooley was right. The sailors supported his work with lavish generosity and cheerfully helped him in his endless scrounging for food, medicine and clothing for the unfortunate Vietnamese.

In his first book, *Deliver Us From Evil,* Dooley related the gentleness with which the American sailors treated the Vietnamese people. On their first trip south more than 2000 refugees were crammed into the *Montague.* The sailors, warned that the Vietnamese might bear contagious diseases, were advised to avoid any physical contact with them. But charity proved stronger than their fears and soon the sailors were right in the midst of the people, dispensing medicine, cleaning sores, and bandaging wounds. These Navy machinists, pipe fitters, and boiler tenders, trained hastily by Dr. Dooley, tended gently some of the most revolting illnesses. "Never once did they betray any emotion other than heartfelt sympathy," Dooley proudly remarked.

If they hid their feelings, the sailors cheerfully displayed great ingenuity. For instance, milk bottles for babies suddenly appeared. No one noticed that the bottles had formerly contained beer (forbidden on Navy vessels at sea). The bottles came complete with nipples supplied from air hoses in the engine room. The tough sailors found themselves babysitting, soothing worried mothers, and joking across the language barriers with the old men.

How much was Tom Dooley responsible for all this? No one knows. The only thing that is sure is that the sailors admired and respected his single-minded devotion to the refugees. Not everyone did. Dr. Dooley had his own style of doing things. He was brash, could be flip, and more than once stepped on sensitive toes. The refugees didn't know that side of him, and surely they didn't care. To them he was the "Good American Doctor."

*   *   *   *   *

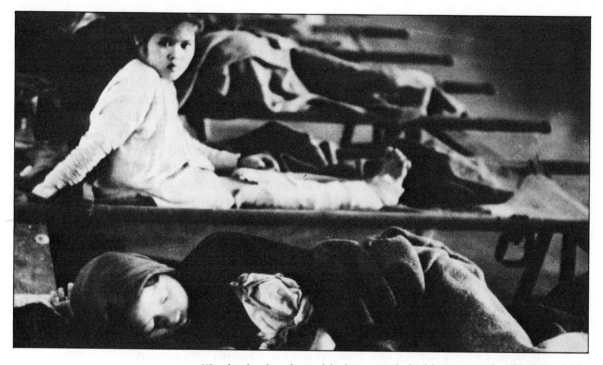

"In the depths of anguish these people had hearts so splendid and a faith so powerful," Dooley wrote of the Vietnamese who were fleeing south on the "Passage to Freedom."

Tom Dooley was no stranger to the cruelties of war. He had lost his brother, Earle, in World War II and had tended the wounded in the naval hospitals. He experienced a period of uncertainty when his younger brother, Malcolm, was flying in the United States Air Force during the Korean conflict.

But in the camp at Haiphong he came face to face, for the first time, with atrocities. The Communists with inhuman ferocity had tortured and maimed many refugees. One day a middle-aged man and a group of first-grade boys and girls struggled into Dooley's clinic. The man's face was swollen beyond recognition; the children had blood and pus flowing from their ears.

An old woman told the doctor their story. Communists had invaded their village and found the man teaching catechism to the youngsters. The soldiers mangled his tongue with a pair of pliers so he could no longer speak the word of God. They then drove chopsticks through the little ones' eardrums so they could never again hear the word of God. It was no wonder Dooley later wrote home, "Mother, I have seen things here I didn't think humans were capable of doing."

In the spring of 1955 the Communists commenced the takeover of Hanoi and Haiphong. Tom Dooley was one of the last Americans to depart Haiphong. Just before leaving, Tom visited the Catholic mission church where he had assisted at daily Mass for the past year. During the course of that year he had come to love a pilgrim statue of Our Lady of Fatima which stood in the church. Years before, the pope had given this statue to a group of Vietnamese Catholics when they visited Rome. Tom, fearful the Communists would desecrate the figure of our Lady, wrapped the statue in an American Aid blanket, drove it to the airport and had it flown to Saigon.

Right after Dooley himself reached Saigon, President Ngo Dinh Diem, then the leader of South Vietnam, summoned him to his office. The young officer could not understand why the president would send for him. Soon after his arrival Dooley found out. President Diem pinned on him the nation's highest award and enrolled him as an officer in the National Order of Vietnam. In his citation President Diem noted: "I have heard your name mentioned often by the refugees. . . . Knowing and loving you, they grew to understand the American people. . . ." Leaving Saigon, Dooley returned to his base in Japan and there received from the United States Navy the Legion of Merit. He was the youngest medical officer in naval history to receive this high honor.

Now, with both tragedy and triumph behind him, the 28-year-old Dr. Dooley looked forward to returning to the United States and his medical career and eventually to marriage and a family. He planned to spend a year in residency at the Naval Hospital in Bethesda, Maryland, studying orthopedics.

His future seemed bright; his plans for it clear and orderly. He had been something of a legend in Vietnam and had every right to expect that his fine reputation would further his naval career. But things were not that simple. Something was gnawing at Dr. Dooley. He was unable to shake the memory of those miserable yet heroic refugees he had served in Haiphong.

Dooley was concerned for more than the people's medical needs. He thoroughly studied the origins of the Vietnam conflict.

It was while he was awaiting his return to the United States from Japan that he began to set down in writing his Vietnam experiences. The result was the best seller, *Deliver Us From Evil*. Near the end of the book Dr. Dooley explains what inspired him to write. It was "that stinking mass of humanity under foreign skies, those miserable and diseased people, who in the depths of anguish had hearts so splendid and a faith so powerful. . . ."

The very last words of *Deliver Us From Evil* suggest that Dooley had not exorcised the memories of Vietnam. He quoted from the poetry of Robert Frost:

The woods are lovely, dark and deep,
But I have promises to keep,
And miles to go before I sleep.

*   *   *   *   *

What were those promises? Did they concern a career as a Navy doctor? Or establishing a private and lucrative practice in the United States? Was there something or someone as yet unclear, undefined, unresolved in his mind and heart? With what spirit was Dr. Dooley wrestling as he attempted to settle down in the States?

Shortly after he returned to the United States, and before starting his studies at Bethesda Naval Hospital, Dooley's superiors, anxious to inform the American public of the Navy's role in Passage to Freedom, sent him on a lecture tour throughout the nation. He spoke before audiences that varied from medical societies to high school assemblies; from tough submariners to hearty Rotarians. Dooley was indefatigable. He often gave two or three lectures in one day, but his message was always the same. "I have seen in Haiphong," he related, "simple, tender, loving medical care—the crudest kind of medicine practiced by my inexperienced medics—change a people's fear and hatred to friendship and understanding. We have witnessed the power of medical aid to reach the hearts and souls of a nation. We have seen it transform the brotherhood of man from an ideal into a reality. . . ." Dooley had learned a great truth in Haiphong, and he tirelessly proclaimed it up and down the land: "The brotherhood of man is as real as the fatherhood of God, . . . and medicine on a person-to-person basis is one of the best means of changing that magnificent phrase from mere words to reality."

Even before he left Haiphong he had toyed with the idea of returning to Southeast Asia. But sometime during these three months of lecturing, the vague idea took sharp focus. And then one day Dr. Dooley told his mother, "I am resigning from the Navy and going to Laos." His mother, brokenhearted that he was once again leaving the country, remembered, "It was as simple as that."

*   *   *   *   *

Tom immediately contacted the former Navy medics who had served so skillfully alongside him at Haiphong—Norman Baker, Peter Kessey and Dennis Shepard—and invited them to join him in his Laotian medical mission. The three young men quickly and cheerfully assented, and by early fall of 1956 they had established a clinic in Vang Vieng, just north of Vientiane, capital of Laos. Dooley was now realizing his dream of practicing person-to-person medicine. The poor, the diseased, the injured, the dying poured out of the jungles to his tiny clinic.

"Many of the children here suffer from some degree of malnutrition, beriberi, and other deficiency diseases. There are the tubercular oldsters and the scabby-headed infants. What a need there is here for medicine," he exulted. He received all with kindness and concern. Both his American and Laotian helpers worked cheerfully and efficiently alongside the man whom the people of the jungle, like the Haiphong refugees, soon came to call "Good American Doctor."

But not everybody appreciated Dr. Dooley. He ran into opposition from two widely divergent sources: the local witch doctors and members of the American colony in Laos. The witch doctors resented his presence because he began attracting their business. Dooley, afraid they might undo his work by exciting fear in his patients, quickly remedied the situation by inviting them in for individual consultation on various patients. "While they were doing their incantations," Dooley remembered, "I could quickly inject a needle. When the cure came and the patient paid his fee—usually a few eggs or a couple of coconuts—I would give half to the witch doctor." Dooley cracked up audiences in the United States by pointing out that the American Medical Association would forbid such a practice. "It is called," noted Dooley dryly, "fee-splitting."

Many members of Laos' American colony judged Dooley an egomaniac whose major concern was personal publicity. One American, newly arrived in Laos, decided to journey up to Vang Vieng to see for himself. He found Dooley indeed a man of mountainous ego—brilliant, impatient with mediocrity, possessing a charm that he could, in the visitor's words, "turn on and off like a spigot." "But the real Dooley emerged," the American remembered, "when he treated the children. His voice would soften, he would almost croon to sick children as he gave them shots of penicillin and quieted them with a stick of candy or a toy balloon. . . . Dooley was a shy, lonely man, ridden by doubts and fears, possessed with the burning desire to help, but fearful that he would be misunderstood. . . ."

A few years later a friend advised Dooley: "Tom, it's good you never married—because despite your great facility with words, you never communicate what's really inside you!" Tom Dooley was indeed an intensely private person and ultimately a very lonely person.

He often disparaged his own talents. But medical experts who visited him and those who worked with him were quick to correct the impression that jungle conditions were such that Dooley could only practice medicine in a primitive manner. "Hmph!" sniffed one visiting doctor, "People on Park Avenue are not getting better treatment or better medicine than Dooley is dispensing in that jungle."

Dooley, despite his hectic career in medical school, developed into a true professional. He ran a tight ship. He would tolerate no sloppiness of dress or carelessness in medical practice from his staff. Any deviation from

Dooley attending an old woman in his Laotian clinic.

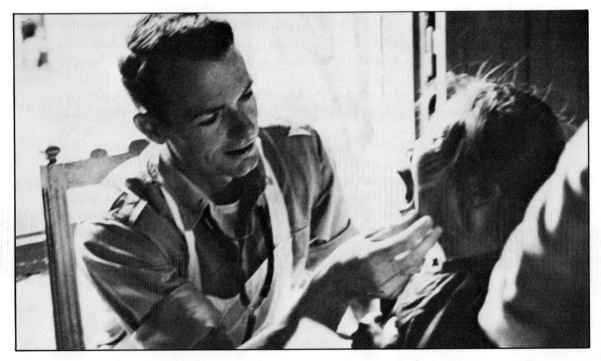

his standards earned his Laotian or American assistants a sharp reprimand. No one was under any illusions about who was boss in the clinic or what the boss demanded—the very best from all of them. Once when the guerilla activity intensified near Dooley's clinic in Laos, the American ambassador suggested that the doctor move the clinic to a less dangerous area. Dooley was upset by the request and that evening wrote home to his mother:

> I am a doctor. This is the root of me—I am a doctor. Everything else, everyone, is second to that. First, I am a doctor. All my duties are entwined with that, and they are clear and lucid. Everything else is secondary. Home life, social life, writing life, living life, loving life, family, friends, romance, fame, fortune, all these are secondary because I am a doctor.

Needless to say, Dooley did not move.

Near the end of his jungle career Dooley proudly advised a visitor one day, "Any one of these youngsters working with me could enter any American medical school on my recommendation."

The extent to which he had won the world's admiration was made clear at the end of 1959 when the Gallup Poll listed him among the world's 10 most admired men. Some of the other men on the poll that year were Winston Churchill, Dwight Eisenhower and Pope John XXIII. How much did it mean to him? He wrote to his mother, "It's a wonderful honor to find that I am the world's seventh most admired man, but it is equally frightening."

*   *   *   *   *

Six months after Dr. Dooley established his first clinic, the Prime Minister of Laos, Prince Souvanna Phouma, asked him if he would pioneer a new clinic at Nam Tha, a village only a short distance from the border of Red China. Delighted, Tom assented. He left his pioneer clinic in the hands of the Laotians he had trained and established his second medical outpost. A few months after the move the clinic was functioning smoothly, and Tom felt free to return to the United States. He came home to put into operation a plan that had been brewing in his head for some time.

In 1958 MEDICO was founded by Dr. Dooley and Dr. Peter Comanduras, a Washington, D.C., physician. At a press conference in February the jungle doctor announced their plan to establish an organization whose purpose was to care for people in areas of the world where medical help was scarce or non-existent. "We actually believe," Dooley said that day, "that we can win the friendship of people only when working beside them, on equal terms, humans to humans, toward goals they understand and seek themselves. MEDICO is a person-to-person, heart-to-heart program."

Over the next five months Tom Dooley gave 188 speeches in 79 cities to publicize his medical program. He spoke with such frequency and intensity that often his tongue blistered. Once more his magic with words worked miracles. Money and supplies poured into MEDICO headquarters in New York. Many young American doctors, nurses and students, touched by Dooley's sincerity and sense of mission, volunteered to join him. Somehow during these whirlwind days he found time to write his second book, *The Edge of Tomorrow*. The work described his medical mission in Laos, and it became an instant best seller. Its proceeds went, of course, to the support of MEDICO.

In the fall of 1958 the triumphant Dr. Dooley returned to pioneer his third medical mission in Laos. He located this clinic in Muong Sing, a tiny village set on the lush green floor of a deep valley in northern Laos. The humble hamlet, surrounded by great dark mountains, reminded him of Shangri-La. But it didn't take Dr. Dooley long to discover that Muong Sing was just another unsanitary, underdeveloped Asian village, alive with sickness and disease.

Soon the clinic's routine was established and long lines of frightened, foul-smelling, diseased people came to receive treatment from the friendly foreign doctor and his Laotian and American helpers. In February 1959 Dooley and his team decided to make a river trip to care for the sick in the mud villages along the Nam Tha River. "It was a journey," Dooley wrote, "into wretchedness, misery, stink, and poverty."

On the 11th day out, Dr. Dooley disembarked from the small boat and climbed up the river bank. As he was climbing he tripped over the lace of his boot and plunged down the bank. He fell about 25 feet and landed on a cluster of rocks set in the bottom of the bank. His rib cage took the brunt of the fall.

The pain remained with him long after he concluded the river trip. Indeed it spread throughout his chest and into his left arm. Dooley never complained—he rarely spoke about it at all—and he continued his punishing schedule. He worked all day and frequently spent the nights studying, writing, and making emergency calls. Whenever possible, he attended Mass before beginning his daily work.

Six months after Dooley's fall, Dr. William Van Valin, a friend of Tom's, visited the Muong Sing clinic. At Tom's request the doctor excised a lump, the size of a golfball, from Dooley's chest. Van Valin, who knew Dooley was an expert diagnostician, showed him the lump after the operation. "It's just a cyst," said Dooley with a sigh of relief. Van Valin insisted on sending the lump to Bangkok for a biopsy. The procedure was routine and Dooley forgot about it.

On August 15, the Feast of the Assumption, 1959, Dr. Dooley received a cable from the director of MEDICO requesting him to return immediately to the United States. Dooley complied. On a stopover at Bangkok he learned the reason for his call home. An associate met him at the airport, brought him to the bar, and said, "Tom, order a stiff bourbon and drink it. I've got some bad news for you." Dooley obeyed. "Now, Tom, I've got to tell you, that lump Van Valin excised was a serious cancer."

Dooley looked at him. "Oh," he said, obviously relieved, "I thought you were going to tell me that something was wrong with my work, or that MEDICO was in trouble, or something like that."

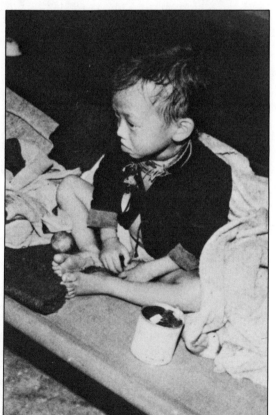

After his first cancer operation, Dooley continued a hectic pace. In the spring of 1960 he lectured 55 times in 30 cities in 34 days.

But Dooley was in trouble. He knew it and accepted it with almost unbelievable calm. Soon after his return to the States he checked into New York City's Memorial Hospital for Cancer. Doctors suggested an operation to remove all possible traces of the disease. CBS Television requested and obtained permission from Tom to televise the operation from first preparation until release by surgeons. Dooley assented to the unusual request because he felt it would help other people in their battle with the disease. A reporter for the now defunct *Look* magazine was astounded by Dooley's calmness amid all the confusion of the preparation for the operation. "He was not reveling in the attention he was receiving," the writer reported, "but he professed not to mind it."

"Look," Dooley advised his visitor, "every time someone snaps my picture, it means six more bottles of cough medicine on my shelf. . . . I'm just an instrument, a tool. I need people to lift me, to give me medicine for the poor."

The reporter noted that Dooley's spirit of dedication was matched by common sense and balance. "The fanatic's gleam is missing from his eyes—the divine madness of the zealot is absent from his manner," the *Look* writer noted. After the operation his doctors advised Tom that as far as they could tell, all traces of the cancer had been removed. When people questioned Dooley about how long he had to live, he simply answered in the words of Walt Whitman, "It is not important what you do with the *years* of your life—but it is how you use each *hour*."

Use each hour he did. Hardly out of the hospital, he began work on his third book, *The Night They Burned the Mountain.* By October he was back on the lecture circuit and within the next two months made 49 speeches in 37 cities and raised almost a million dollars for MEDICO. St. Louis Jaycees purchased an $18,000 airplane to enable Dooley to fly to his clinics in Southeast Asia as well as contact the new MEDICO clinics that were now springing up in Asia.

On Christmas Day he flew into Muong Sing, his plane full of supplies for the clinic and gifts for the staff and village children. Although he suffered a severe bout of malaria, he was soon back at work. On January 18 he wrote home:

I must go into the burnt soil of my personal mountain of sadness, plant the new seedlings of my life. I must continue to live. I must cultivate my fields of food to feed those who cannot feed themselves. . . . The jagged ugly cancer scar goes no deeper than my flesh. There is no cancer in my spirit. The Lord saw to that.

Quoting Camus, Dooley went on:

"In the midst of winter, I suddenly found that there was in me an invincible summer." Maybe I could now be tender in a better way. I was a member of the fellowship of those who bear the mark of pain.

He bore the marks of his own pain with silence and dignity, never ceasing the pace of the work, never permitting the cancer to hinder his medical practice. At times he refused to take the pain-killing drugs ordered by his physicians lest in performing surgery his mind would be clouded or his reflexes slowed.

He opened a new clinic at Ban Houei Sai and continued work on his book. MEDICO now had 17 projects going in 12 countries, and Dooley had a hand, one way or another, in establishing each of them.

In May he returned to the United States, and a checkup at Memorial assured him that the cancer had not spread. But he wasn't fooled. He told a doctor who planned to return to Laos with him that he felt he had eight to ten months to live. "He said it with such simplicity," the doctor recalled, "that I was speechless."

*   *   *   *   *

By the end of the summer Dr. Dooley was back in Laos and, if anything, accelerated his activity. He was everywhere, visiting his clinics, recruiting personnel, moving supplies through customs, practicing in his clinics, operating, flying to various parts of Southeast Asia on MEDICO projects. He was in a pitiless race against time.

In October he made a quick trip back to the States for another checkup and within a few weeks was back in Asia. He drove himself mercilessly. His friends tried to get him to slow down, but he refused. "I have so

When the University of Notre Dame conferred an honorary degree on him in 1960, President Eisenhower, the commencement speaker, paid him tribute for his courage, self-sacrifice and faith.

much to do and so little time.'' By late November Tom knew that his end was near. As the cancer metastasized into his spine the pain became severe. Walking became difficult. He was wearing a back brace. He called it ''the Iron Maiden'' and hoped it would enable him to walk a little better. Despite all, he continued his usual pace, still exhausting far healthier people who worked for him. He convinced all about him that he had his medical problems under control. Only a very few people knew that, hidden from the eyes of all, the cheerful face of Tom Dooley froze in pain and his smiling Irish eyes filled with tears.

His last trip through Southeast Asia, journeying from clinic to clinic, from friend to friend, still recruiting, still purchasing drugs, still selling MEDICO, still visiting doctors, was a modern-day Way of the Cross. He kept saying, ''I must go on. I simply must.'' But from time to time the illness flattened him. In early December he wound up in the hospital in Hong Kong. There he wrote a beautiful letter to Father Hesburgh, president of Notre Dame. Speaking in almost mystical terms of his sufferings, Dooley acknowledged that the fierce pain almost overwhelmed him.

> But yet a milder storm of peace gathers in my heart. What seems unpossessable, I can possess. What seems unfathomable, I fathom. What is unutterable, I can utter. Because I can pray. I can communicate. How do people endure anything on earth if they cannot have God?

Dr. Dooley had written to Father Hesburgh because he was journeying in his mind back to the Grotto of Our Lady at Notre Dame.

> How I long for the Grotto. Away from the Grotto Dooley just prays. But at the Grotto, especially now, when there must be snow everywhere, and the lake is ice glass and that triangular fountain on the left is frozen solid and all the priests are bundled in their too-large, too-long, old black coats, and the students wear snow boots . . .; if I could go to the Grotto now, then I think I could sing inside. I could be full of faith and poetry and loveliness and know more beauty, tenderness and compassion. This is soggy sentimentalism, I know. (Old prayers from a hospital bed are just as pleasing to God as more youthful prayers from a Grotto on the lid of night.)''

*   *   *   *   *

A few days before Christmas Dooley checked into a hotel in Bangkok. He called a local Redemptorist priest and asked for communion. The priest found Dooley lying on a mattress on the floor of his hotel room, his brace beside him, clutching a rosary. "Tom, you should go to a hospital," the priest advised.

Dooley shrugged, "They can't do anything for me—I'll be flying home very soon."

On Christmas Day the priest visited Tom again and wished him a merry Christmas. Tom responded gently, "It really isn't a very merry Christmas, is it, Father? But if this is the way God wants it to be, that is the way I want it, too." Then Dr. Dooley received communion with deep emotion and wept softly. The priest later wrote that Dooley reminded him of Christ, who, at the same age as Dooley, saw the end of his mission approaching and prayed in the Garden of Gethsemane, "Father, if it is your will, let this chalice pass from me—nevertheless, not my will, but thine, be done."

On Christmas Day Tom Dooley, walking with a limp and bent over in pain, boarded the Boeing 707 that would fly him home. In a last display of iron determination he refused a wheelchair and walked to the plane unaided. The big jet sped down the runway and slowly climbed into the sky, carrying Tom Dooley from Southeast Asia for the last time.

Dr. Dooley reached New York in a December snowstorm and died peacefully at Memorial Hospital on January 18, 1961, one day after his 34th birthday. Tom Dooley had no more miles to walk—no more promises to keep. He had passed through his woods, lovely, dark and deep.

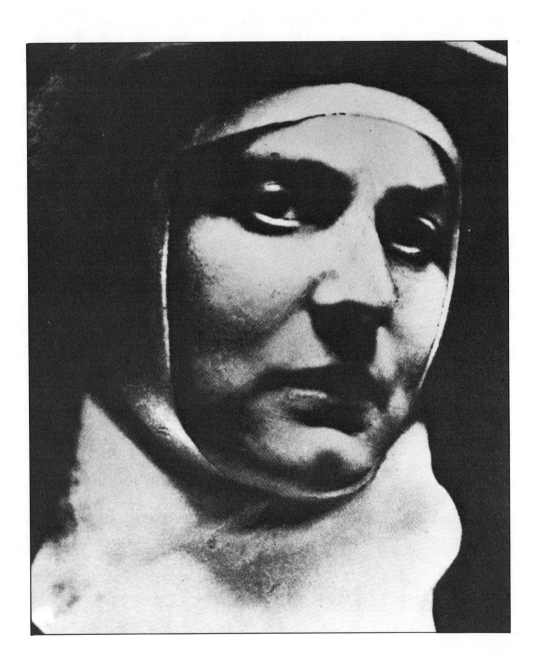

Edith Stein

"Aunt Edith, why now?" The 12-year-old's face had suddenly become as grave as an adult's. Her eyes, clear and solemn, gazed steadily at the face of the older woman and clearly indicated the young girl's insistence on an answer.

"Little one," the aunt, a woman in her early 40s, answered, "I have been waiting for 11 years to take this step. Now I can. The hour is late."

"But, Aunt," the niece countered, "a nun. . . . I don't understand."

"It is hard to understand," Aunt Edith responded. "Let me try to explain. . . . We are both of us born Jews. I became a Catholic 11 years ago but I still am a Jew. Our people, little one, are now in serious danger. I want to offer my life as a cloistered nun for them."

The girl neither understood the danger to which Edith referred, nor how entering a cloister could help Jews. But she loved Aunt Edith and accepted her word.

The rest of Edith's immediate family, the Steins, and her many relatives were not that indulgent. They were distressed when the 31-year-old Edith was baptized in the Catholic church at Bergzabern in her native Germany in 1922. Eleven years after that shock, the news that the brilliant and accomplished Edith intended to bury herself in a cloister bewildered and saddened them. The move, however, did not surprise them. The Steins knew Edith as one who could and often did break the mold. Clear-headed, highly intelligent and disciplined, she often set outrageously high goals for herself and achieved them. She possessed a wide range of talents—all of them controlled by her considerable inner strength. Edith Stein's qualities were no accidents; in all of them she was very much her mother's child.

*   *   *   *   *

Frau Auguste Stein, mother of seven, was widowed in 1893 when her youngest child, Edith, was just two years old. Her late husband had owned a growing lumber business in Breslau, Germany. At the time of his death the business was not going well. It needed a firm hand and knowledgeable head to guide it. Frau Stein provided both. It mattered little that she knew next to nothing about lumber when she took over the business. It mattered even less to the indomitable Frau that the traditional areas of responsibility for a middle-class German housewife were church or synagogue, children and kitchen. The widow was completely willing to make any sacrifice, ex-

Edith, left, and a younger sister.

perience any danger or discomfort to protect, nourish and educate the little ones God gave her. So quickly and thoroughly did she learn the timber trade that within a short time she won the respect of others in the business. She so mastered her trade that she could calculate from the window of a speeding railroad car the value of a stand of trees in a forest.

A Jewish mother, Frau Stein observed the traditions of her faith at home, in the synagogue and in her business life. She thanked God for the energy and talent to earn the necessities of life for her family. As far as money was concerned, she observed the ancient Jewish tradition: To be happy with money, you must save a little, spend a little and give a little! Frau Stein gave a lot to the poor, to fellow businessmen having bad luck, or to any of her numerous relatives in financial difficulties. She said little about her benefactions.

*   *   *   *   *

Edith was born on the Jewish Day of the Atonement, October 12, 1891. Frau Stein and the older sons and daughters lavished great affection on the baby. Lively and bright, Edith brought joy to the whole family. She romped cheerfully about the Stein home with her sister, Erna, 18 months older than herself. Her oldest brother began training her memory at an early age, and by the time she was four years old Edith could recite lists of German literary works and their authors. She and Erna joined their playmates at games and children's parties. Frau Stein particularly enjoyed watching them play hide-and-go-seek amid the woodpiles in the family lumberyard.

When Erna went off to grammar school, Edith, furious because she was too young to accompany her, threw a temper tantrum. No amount of footstamping or tears, however, could bend stern Prussian law which held that a child had to be six years of age to enter school. To keep peace Frau Stein sent Edith to kindergarten. The teacher, realizing Edith's precociousness, soon requested that the little girl remain at home until she could enter primary school.

Relieved to be out of kindergarten and still determined to enter primary school, Edith arranged through her older sister, Else, a licensed

Auguste and Siegfried Stein had 11 children, four of whom died as babies.
Edith sits in the front, second from the right.

teacher, to enter first grade the moment she was six. Since the Prussian school term began at Easter, Edith entered on October 12, 1897—six months behind her class. By Christmas she was near the top of the first grade.

This first school year set the pattern of Edith's entire scholastic life. Brilliant, disciplined, ambitious, she gained many honors but rarely top honors. She was a Jew; and Jews, even at that time in Germany, were victimized by a muted but effective anti-Semitism.

*   *   *   *   *

At 19 Edith entered the University of Breslau, taking her major in philosophy. It was rare enough in those days for women to pursue doctoral studies; it was even more rare for them to enter a discipline as abstract as philosophy. Edith chose the field because she judged philosophy to be the vehicle by which she could discover the truth about herself and the world about her. She preferred philosophy to religion, which she had judged in her early teens as incapable of leading her to truth. No longer believing in a personal God, she observed the external practices of Judaism only to placate her mother. Inwardly she was an agnostic.

The young student conducted her personal search for truth with characteristic intensity. "The pursuit of truth," she later remarked, "was my only passion." Her studies led her again and again to the work of Dr. Edmund Husserl, a brilliant German-Jewish philosopher who taught at the University of Goettingen. So dedicated was she to her ideal that she transferred from the University of Breslau and enrolled at Goettingen to study

The Stein home in Breslau, Germany, where Edith was born on Oct. 17, 1891.

with Husserl, the great master, himself. It did not take long for the 54-year-old Husserl to recognize her brilliance.

If the pursuit of truth was her only passion, it was not her only interest. Edith loved the outdoors and thoroughly enjoyed hiking through the forests and mountains of Germany with her fellow students. And sometime during her student career she apparently fell in love. She discreetly avoided mentioning the name of the young man, except to say that she hoped that someday he would be her husband. For whatever reason, the relationship never developed. Its conclusion had its effects on the young philosopher. She wrote that it left her "very unwell; my suffering was due to the interior struggles I was experiencing unknown to anyone and without help." It wasn't that Edith lacked friends. "She had," a contemporary wrote, "a genius for friendship." But apparently no one within the large circle of her friends could help her through this trial of disappointed love.

In 1915, the second year of World War I, Edith and some of her fellow students volunteered to serve in a hospital in Moravia. The young philosopher notified her mother that she planned to take time off from her studies to serve as a Red Cross nurse in a hospital that cared for Austrian soldiers who had contracted various contagious diseases. Frau Stein replied to her starry-eyed daughter: "I forbid this. These soldiers are not only ill but are covered with lice when they return from the front. Edith, you'll not go with my permission." It was a clear matriarchal command.

"Then," wrote back hardheaded Edith, "I shall have to go without your permission." Edith was indeed her mother's daughter.

The little troop of university women set off cheerfully to serve the ill soldiers. "Registered nurses, our superiors, did not make the work easy for us," one of the women wrote, "probably because they wanted to show us that our 'higher education' at the university was not worth much in comparison with their knowledge of nursing." She added, "They were probably right."

When her six months of duty as a Red Cross nurse ended, Edith returned to the university. She resumed her work with Husserl and, when he accepted the chair of philosophy at the University of Freiburg in 1916, she accepted his invitation to accompany him there. That same year she earned her doctorate, and Professor Husserl appointed her to be his personal teaching assistant and charged her with putting his voluminous writings in order.

Edith remained at Freiburg until 1919. She had hoped to obtain a teaching position at Goettingen, but failed. She then returned to her home at Breslau.

* * * * *

Two episodes—unrelated, unplanned and unconnected with her philosophical studies—combined to encourage Edith to take a radical new direction in her pilgrimage toward truth.

The first occurred late in 1917 when Dr. Husserl sent her to represent him at the funeral of a mutual colleague, Professor Adolf Reinach, who had been killed at the front. Edith had known Reinach since 1913. She had met him upon her arrival at Goettingen. He was then 30, a Jew, just married and deeply devoted to his wife. The Reinachs, a kindly and cordial couple, took an immediate liking to Husserl's new disciple. Edith, who treasured her memories of the kindly and gentle Adolf, dreaded meeting his bereaved wife. She had nonetheless agreed to Husserl's request and journeyed to Goettingen to attend Adolf's funeral. Her worst fears never materialized. "Frau Reinach," she later recalled, "became a consolation to us instead of our being a consolation to her."

"What is the source of the young widow's strength?" Edith wondered. She knew, of course, that the Reinachs had been baptized in the Lutheran church the year preceding Adolf's death. Frau Reinach, in simplest and gentlest terms, explained to Edith that it was this very Christian faith that strengthened her. "I accept fully in my heart that Adolf now lives with God. He has reached his goal," she exclaimed. Frau Reinach was, of course, in shock when the news first arrived of her beloved husband's death. But she was able to view the terrible tragedy in the perspective of her belief in the resurrection of Christ. "It is my duty now," she said to Edith, "to accept my loss and my portion of the cross of Christ which brings healing and life to men."

Frau Reinach asked Edith to arrange her late husband's philosophical papers. In the course of this work, Dr. Stein came across many references the professor had made to his own search for truth. She was amazed to read Adolf's continual references to prayer as a means for discovering truth. "Through prayer," he had written, "I am in contact with the ultimate background of the world!" It was clear to Edith that Reinach accepted God as truth, Christ as God, and prayer as the most direct path to the source of light and truth.

Reinach's writings threw Edith into intellectual and spiritual turmoil. They led her to consider seriously the role of religion in human experience and to begin a study of Christianity. There is evidence that she began to pray and some indication that she underwent a type of mystical experience. The interior struggle between faith and unbelief was intense and prolonged. For three years Edith waged war within herself. It wasn't until the summer of 1921 that the first signs of peace appeared.

That summer Edith spent a vacation with Herr and Frau Conrad-Martius, a university couple who had befriended her. They owned a farm at Bergzabern and invited Edith to spend her summer holidays with them. One evening when the hosts were away, she sought a book from the library to while away the evening. *The Autobiography of St. Teresa of Avila* caught her eye, and she settled down to read. Teresa's exquisite and disarmingly candid account of her own search for truth immediately cap-

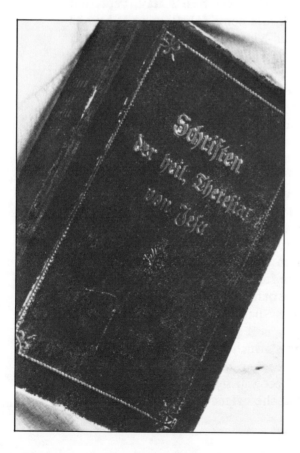

The actual copy of the autobiography of St. Teresa of Avila. Reading the book influenced her struggle to become a Christian.

tivated Edith. She did not go to bed that night until she had finished the book. Teresa, the great Doctor of the Church, sounded the same themes as Reinach—that Christ is the way, the truth and the light, and draws us to himself in prayer. He not only teaches us truth, but helps us live it through union with him.

Shortly before her death, Edith looked back on the days following Reinach's death and her encounter with St. Teresa:

> This was my first encounter with the Cross and with the supernatural strength which it gives. For the first time I saw the redemptive suffering of Christ overcoming death. This was the moment when my unbelief broke down and Christ appeared to me in the mystery of the Cross.

Edith determined to embrace Christianity. On New Year's Day, 1922, she was baptized and took Teresa as her baptismal name. The bishop of Speyer gave special permission for Hedwig Conrad-Martius, a Protestant, to be her godmother.

*   *   *   *   *

Edith had been living at home in Breslau since she left the University of Freiburg in 1919 and had been engaged in scholarly research and writing. Her family did not know of her conversion to Catholicism, but by the spring of 1922 she felt she could no longer conceal her new life from her mother. When she told Frau Stein that she had become a Christian, that good and noble woman bowed her head and wept. Kneeling beside her, Edith too broke down. The tears of the two women mingled. "What," Edith must have thought, "would Mama do if she knew I was considering becoming a nun?" Already the idea was forming in Edith's mind. Her mother did suspect and began warning the rest of the family that the full consequences of Edith's incomprehensible turn to Christianity had not yet appeared.

The following year the Dominican Sisters offered Edith a teaching position as professor of German at their college for girls in Speyer. The Mother Superior quickly recognized Edith's vast talents and broadened her field of activity. She assigned her, a born teacher, to provide teacher-training courses to Dominican teaching nuns. Recognizing Edith's firm grasp of Catholic doctrine, she also requested that she offer religious instructions to

Edith, second from left in the first row, with university friends.

candidates for the Dominican sisterhood. Edith undertook all this extra work cheerfully and refused any salary at all. Besides her classroom duties she continued her scholarly research, translating the letters of Cardinal Newman from English into German and the work, *St. Thomas, Disputed Questions of Truth,* from Latin into German.

Her pupils, the nuns and young women of the college, adored her. Although naturally quiet, Edith possessed a joyous spirit. "She gave us everything," one young woman remembered. "We were very young, but none of us has forgotten her fascinating personality. When she criticized us, she was just."

The youth of Germany at this time needed much kindness and justice. An atmosphere of crisis, despair and disorder shrouded the tortured land. Having rejected the values which brought pre-war Germany to world prominence and then to crushing, humiliating defeat, the youth lived in a spiritual vacuum. In the early '20s no system of values attracted them. Well aware of the cynicism of Germany's young people, Edith wrote:

> The most important point is that women teachers carry the spirit of Christ in their hearts and act it out. . . . But teachers also have a duty to experience the life into which the children later enter. Today's younger generation cannot understand us, but we must try to understand them. Only then can we help them a little.

Life at Speyer suited the new professor. Despite her intense activity, she spent hours at prayer each day. For Edith, prayer was the root of all her work.

> Heaven has a special kind of economy. I do not lengthen my working hours by any tricks. All I need is a quiet corner where I can talk to God each day as if there were nothing else to do. I try to make myself a tool for God. Not for myself, but only for Him.

Canon Schwind of the cathedral staff at Speyer profoundly influenced Edith's spiritual development. The canon, an elderly man, introduced her to a number of friends shortly after her conversion. He was concerned that the young professor should feel welcome in the church and make new acquaintances. He instructed her in the use of the church's

Frau Stein, Edith's mother, could not understand her daughter's conversion to Christianity, much less her decision to become a nun.

daily prayer, the Divine Office, which the new convert recited in Latin. "His spiritual guidance was delicate and bold at the same time," Edith commented. "His confidence in Divine Providence," she added, "was unshakable."

Edith delighted and challenged the canon. "Oh, this philosopher," he once exclaimed, "she asks more questions than ten theologians can answer." To her repeated request to enter the Carmelite cloister, Canon Schwind invariably answered no. "You, Edith, are too young in the faith to take such a step," he advised. "Besides, the work you are doing in Germany's intellectual circles is invaluable to the church." And then he added, "There is a third reason. . . . Your mother is not yet ready for this."

In the fall of 1927 her beloved Canon Schwind died suddenly. After his death Edith wrote:

> He knew how to educate and could give consolation and
> quietude where all other human consolation failed. Strictness
> and kindness, seriousness and childlike cheerfulness,
> grandeur and humility, all these qualities were united in him,
> rooted in his pure love of God.

The following spring, Archabbot Raphael Walzer of the Benedictine Monastery of Beuron became Edith's spiritual mentor.

Brother Maunz, porter of the Beuron Abbey from 1922 to 1933, recalled Edith as "very modest in her words, her manner, her dress, her hairdo. . . . She was so thankful for whatever small favors I did for her." The archabbot remembered her as "a woman sensitive and motherly, simple with simple people and scholarly with scholars . . . seeking with those who were seeking, and, I would almost like to add, a sinner with the sinful. . . ." To Edith's entreaty to enter the Carmelites in Cologne, the abbot responded in the same fashion as Canon Schwind and for precisely the same reasons.

After seven years of teaching, counselling and scholarly research at Speyer, Edith undertook another apostolate. At the request of Father Przwara, S.J., she toured Germany, Switzerland and Austria, lecturing on the importance of women in contemporary life. The imperturbable and clear-sighted philosopher shrank from no aspect of the role of women in the depression years of pre-Hitler Germany. She discoursed on a wide range of topics that included "The Vocations of Men and Women in the Order of

Nature and Grace,'' ''The Life of the Christian Woman,'' ''Fundamental Women's Education,'' ''Woman's Task as Leader of Youth in the Church.''

Edith Stein was not afraid to address the question of women's proper role in the church. She wrote:

> As far as women priests are concerned, it seems to me, doctrinally, that there are no obstacles to prevent the church from introducing such an unheard-of novelty. But in practice there are many reasons for and against.

People who came to hear a radical were disappointed. More often than not, even the clergy were delighted with her talks. ''She spoke without rhetoric,'' one who heard her reported. ''You felt immediately a spiritual strength, a disciplined mind.''

Edith called upon the women of Germany to take their proper role in society. ''Our nation needs us women,'' she insisted, ''not because of what we have; it needs what we are.'' If her messages were not always accepted, they were well received. Many clergy realized that Dr. Stein was a natural leader equipped with marvelous talent which could well serve the church in these difficult years in Germany.

In 1931 Edith concluded her work at the Dominican school at Speyer and returned home to Breslau. She applied for a faculty position at the University of Breslau and at the University of Freiburg. Authorities at both institutions rejected her applications—not, she later learned, because she was a woman but because she was a Jew. The Nazi Party, although it had not yet seized power, had already begun to whip up the latent anti-Semitism which characterized pre-war Germany.

In 1932 Edith managed to obtain a position as an assistant lecturer at the Catholic Institute for Scientific Pedagogy at Muenster.

When Hitler took control of Germany in 1933, anti-Semitism escalated in the Muenster area. Violence was not unknown. After a particularly vicious outbreak of anti-Semitic activity, Edith made a holy hour in the Carmelite convent in Cologne. The holy hour devotion centers on the agony of Christ in the Garden of Gethsemane. During Edith's time at prayer the words of Pascal, the French philosopher, kept repeating themselves in her mind. ''Jesus,'' Pascal had written, ''is in agony until the end of the world.'' Edith recalled:

I said to the Lord as the words kept repeating themselves in my mind that it was his cross that was now laid on the Jewish people. Most of my people did not understand that, but those who did had to bear it willingly in the name of all the others. I wanted to do that, if only he would show me how. . . . When the service came to an end I felt that my wish had been granted. But in what way this bearing of the cross would happen, I still did not know.

Anti-Semitism at Muenster escalated to such a degree that Edith feared her presence on the faculty of the Catholic Institute would incite Nazi wrath against the whole school. "I cannot stay," she advised her spiritual director, Abbot Walzer. "I will only bring harm." Then she added: "For more than a decade, I have wished to enter the Carmelites. Because I am a

Jew, I cannot now find work in Germany. Please, Abbot, does this not seem to be a sign from God, that my work for the church as a lecturer, teacher and writer is now concluded and God is calling me to follow a different path?" She pleaded, "May I go now to Carmel?"

"You have received offers for jobs in South America and other parts of the world," the abbot reminded her.

"I do not wish to leave my people," Edith retorted.

"Then, Edith," the abbot replied, "there is no reason for you not to go to Carmel. This political regime will only be cast out by prayer and fasting. Carmel will offer you plenty of both."

Because she was Jewish, no state university would employ her. In 1932, Edith joined the Catholic Institute at Muenster.

When Edith advised her mother of her decision to enter Carmel, Frau Stein's response was predictable. She wept repeatedly. She pleaded with Edith, in the name of her love for her mother, not to take this step. Frau Stein was 84. It was incomprehensible to her that Edith would become a nun, especially in light of the nascent persecution under the Hitler regime. Frau Stein judged that her beloved Edith was deserting the family in time of serious need. The elderly lady, who had worked so hard to protect her family when her husband died, felt that Edith was denying everything she had taught her.

"My last day at home," Edith wrote, "October 12th, was a Jewish feast day and my birthday." Edith and Frau Stein took a tram to the synagogue and heard the rabbi deliver a "fine sermon." After the service 84-year-old Mama insisted on walking home with her daughter. "It is a 45-minute walk, Mama," Edith reminded her.

"It will do us both good," the indomitable Frau responded.

On the way, the painful question of Edith's entrance into the Carmel came up. The mother said to the daughter: "I have nothing against Christ. It is possible that he was a very good man. But why did he have to make himself God?"

During the afternoon, many relatives and friends came to visit the Steins. Edith welcomed the company since it distracted attention from her. She described the event:

> However, as one after the other left, the family atmosphere became heavy. At the end, Mama and I were left alone in the room. My sisters were busy cleaning up and doing the dishes. She sat down then, placed her head between her hands and began to weep. I slid behind her chair and, taking that precious head with the white hair between my hands, I pressed it against my heart. We remained thus for a long time, until it was time to retire. I took Mama to her room and, for the first time in my life, helped her to undress. Then I sat on her bed. Finally, she sent me to rest. Neither of us slept that night.

Edith remembered going to Mass by herself in the morning and returning home for breakfast. The family sat around the table. Mama tried to eat but could do nothing but weep. Edith recalled:

When Edith entered the Carmelite Cloister at Cologne she wrote, "I entered the house in deepest peace."

I came over to her and held her close until it was time to leave. Then I motioned to Erna, my sister, to take my place until I went to put on my coat and hat in an adjoining room. At last came the goodbyes. Mama embraced me tenderly. Erna said to me, "The Eternal One be with you." Just as I embraced Erna, Mama began to weep aloud. I went out quickly, accompanied by Rosa and Else (two of Edith's sisters). No one leaned from the window to wave to me as was our custom.

Rosa and Else accompanied her to the train station. As the Cologne-bound train pulled in, the sisters exchanged tearful farewells. Finally Edith boarded the coach and waved farewell from the window.

This was the start, in October 1933, of a new stage in Edith's search for truth.

* * * * *

Edith Stein

Although 42, a doctor of philosophy and a renowned writer and lecturer, the independent Edith adapted rather well to the prayer, silence, work and gentle recreation that characterized the life of the Carmelite nuns in Cologne. Her fellow postulants had little idea of who she was in the world, and neither they nor she cared very much about the past. The only clue she gave of her former professional status was her inexperience in housework. Her novice mistress unfailingly corrected her housekeeping inadequacies—a kindness Edith, who had received many honors in the academic world, deeply appreciated. On April 15, 1934, Carmelite superiors gave formal permission for Edith to be clothed in the religious habit. To symbolize her new life and mission she took a new name, Sister Teresa Benedicta of the Cross. By her formal entrance into the novitiate, she took a significant step toward realizing the purpose of her life—to suffer with Jesus for her people so that they might be saved and rise to new life.

She radiated a quiet joy. "If something is given to you for which you have prayed a long time, this fulfillment is then almost more over-

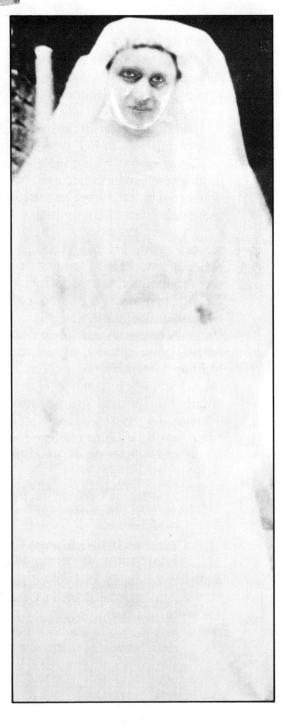

At age 42, a doctor of philosophy and a recognized writer and lecturer, Edith Stein became a postulant at Carmel.

whelming than an instant granting,'' she wrote of her long years of waiting to
enter Carmel. The only cloud on her horizon was her mother's refusal to
answer her letters. But eventually Frau Stein overcame her hurt and resumed
correspondence.

Edith's superiors encouraged her to resume her scholarly writings and
gave permission for her to receive visitors at the grille. All these activities had
to be carried out within the constraints of the Carmelite daily routine. Her
most severe penances occurred when she had to break the intense concentration her scholarly work required to answer the bell (the ''voice of God'')
summoning her to community exercises, meals or recreation.

Sister Benedicta's scholarly labors centered around her attempt to
reconcile the philosophy of St. Thomas Aquinas with contemporary
philosophies, which she had begun some time before entering Carmel. The
task required an immense effort. She entitled the work *Finite and Eternal Being*. She completed it in 1936, only to find that no publisher would accept it
because its authoress was a Jew.

Along with her philosophical work, Edith produced a number of
religious and spiritual essays and books. Her spiritual writings are clear,
lucid and scholarly, yet written in terms the ordinary reader can grasp. Her
literary work before and after she entered the Carmel covered a vast field. In
addition to spiritual writings and her three major philosophical works—*St.
Thomas, Disputed Questions of Truth; Finite and Eternal Being;* and *Contributions to a Philosophical Foundation of Psychology*—Edith authored
books and articles on mystical theology and social questions current in the
Germany of her day.

Much of her spiritual writing centered about the theme of the light
shining in the darkness. In a powerful essay entitled ''The Mystery of
Christmas,'' she reflected:

> The Son of the Eternal Father descended from the glory of
> Heaven because the mystery of Iniquity had shrouded the
> earth in the darkness of night.
>   Darkness covered the earth and He came as the light
> that shines in the darkness, but the darkness did not com-
> prehend Him. To those who receive Him, He brought light
> and peace; peace with the Father in Heaven, peace with all
> those who, like them, are children of light and children of the

Father in Heaven; peace also in the intimate depths of the heart. But no peace for the children of darkness. To them the Prince of Peace does not bring peace, but the sword. To them He is the stumbling block against which they knock and on which they are broken. This is a bitterly serious truth which ought not to be obscured by the poetic charm of the Child in the Manger. The mystery of the Incarnation is closely linked to the mystery of Iniquity. The night of sin appears all the more black and uncanny against the light that has come down from Heaven.

In another essay entitled "The Prayer of the Church," Edith revealed the very heart of her belief in the significance of prayer—private prayer and the mystical prayer of contemplatives as well as liturgical prayer—in the work of redemption. She wrote of the Jewish high priest who went alone,

The monastery garden provided the tranquillity she craved.

once a year, into the Jerusalem Temple's most sacred area, the Holy of Holies. There the priest, a sinner himself, stood before the Lord to pray for his people. She described Christ, the sinless high priest who spent long nights in silent prayer, continuing the tradition of the Jewish high priest. She depicted the Lord as reaching the epitome of silent worship in the terrible hour of solitude, suffering and surrender of Gethsemane.

She also wrote:

> In the hiddenness of the quiet chamber of Nazareth, the power of the Holy Ghost came upon the Virgin praying in solitude, and brought about the Incarnation of the Savior. Assembled around the silently praying Virgin, the nascent Church awaited the promise, the coming of the Holy Ghost that was to vivify them unto inner enlightenment and fruitful external activity. In the night of blindness that God had laid on his eyes, Saul awaited in solitary prayer the answer of the Lord to his question, "What will you have me to do?" In solitary prayer Peter was prepared for his mission to the Gentiles. And so it remains through the centuries. In the solitary conversation of consecrated souls there are prepared those widely visible events of the Church's history that renew the face of the earth.

In another essay, "Inner Life and External Form and Action," she wrote:

> The mystical stream (of prayer), which flows through all the centuries, is no spurious side-current that has strayed from the prayer life of the Church—it is her very life blood.

*   *   *   *   *

Following her one-year novitiate, Sister Benedicta pronounced her first profession of vows in April 1935. Her calm and serenity deepened. Her faithful friend, Hedwig Conrad-Martius, visited her shortly after the profession. Hedwig remembered:

> The hour of our meeting stands clearly before me. Edith always had something childlike and friendly about her. But the feeling of being sheltered and the inner bliss which she had reached were, if I may say so, enchanting. Edith told me during this meeting that she had some difficulties during her

first year of novitiate, but she had overcome them and how much she had won!

A year following her profession of vows, Edith received word that her mother, who had never been seriously ill in her life, was suffering from possible stomach cancer. Doctors could do little except keep her as comfortable as possible. She bore her illness with strong-willed compusure and resignation. One thing alone she could not understand. "Why," she inquired of the family, "cannot Edith be with her mother?" On her part, Edith felt deeply the pain of separation. "My poor mother," she wrote a friend, "please pray for her. . . . It is very hard and incomprehensible to her that I cannot be with her."

On September 14, 1936, Edith renewed her vows. At precisely the hour she did this, her mother went to her eternal reward.

"When I renewed my vows," Edith told a fellow Carmelite, "my mother was with me. I distinctly felt her presence."

Edith's sister Rosa was baptized in the Catholic Church following their mother's death. For a time she lived at the Cologne convent outside the enclosure.

Two years later, Edith's mentor, Dr. Husserl, lay dying in a Catholic convent. He had taken refuge there with his wife after the Nazis banned him from the classroom and lecture hall. One of his former students, Benedictine Sister Adelgundis, arranged for the Husserls to come to the convent of St. Lioba. Husserl fell ill. On Good Friday, 1938, he seemed to undergo some kind of mystical experience. He kept moving his arms in the bed as if to protect himself from some terrifying force. When he was asked what it was, he replied, "Light and darkness—much darkness and again light." Before his death on April 27, 1938, he had another such experience. He told Sister Adelgundis that he had seen something wonderful and asked her to write it down. Before the nun had time to fetch paper and pencil, Husserl was dead.

*   *   *   *   *

During the nights of November 9 and 10, Nazi mobs stormed through the streets of Germany, burning, looting, beating and murdering Jews. Jewish homes, property and synagogues were broken into and pillaged. The nation had gone mad. "This is the shadow of the Cross falling on my people," Edith wrote. "Woe also to this city and this country when God shall revenge what is today done to the Jews."

Edith, convinced along with her superiors that her presence would bring Nazi wrath upon the innocent nuns of Cologne, was given permission to emigrate to the Carmelite convent in Echt, Holland. She was joined there by her sister Rosa in the summer of 1940.

German forces invaded and occupied Holland in 1940. The Stein sisters were in grave peril. Carmelite authorities attempted to transfer them to a Swiss Carmel. Negotiations, however, grew complicated and ultimately defied resolution.

The Nazis continued their persecution of the Jews in Holland. Hitler decreed that every Jewish child be expelled from Dutch schools and citizens of Jewish origin be prohibited from holding public office. The Gestapo, Hitler's secret police, hunted down, arrested and deported thousands of Jews

For the safety of the sisters in Cologne, Edith sought refuge with the sisters of Carmel in Echt, Holland. "They received me with great kindness," she wrote.

to the dreaded concentration camps, gas chambers and crematory ovens.

The Dutch people protested. Brave, non-Jewish Hollanders wore on their clothing the infamous yellow star the Nazis required all Jews to wear. In July 1942 Dutch Catholic bishops wrote a pastoral letter condemning Nazi actions against the Jews. In retaliation the Gestapo dragnet swept across the face of Holland, enmeshing any person with the slightest trace of Jewish blood. Catholic priests and religious of Jewish parents were particular targets of Nazi wrath.

Two officers came to the Echt Carmel and arrested Edith and Rosa. Word of the arrest spread quickly through the neighborhood. Dutch men and women rallied in support of the sisters in front of the Carmel, but to no avail. The Stein sisters were herded into a police van. It was the start of their journey to a death camp in the East.

During her three years at Echt, Edith worked on two treatises on mystical theology. In one, "Science of the Cross," she had written: "The Crucified demands that we should follow Him. . . . that He who formed

In her room in Echt, Edith wrote reflections on the Passion of Christ and continued her scholarly research.

Himself had permitted Himself to be formed into the image of the Cross Bearer.'' Edith herself would be formed into the image of the Cross Bearer.

The Gestapo shipped the latest group of victims, including Rosa and Edith, to Westerbork, Holland, an assembly point where the Nazis organized transportation to the concentration camps in the East. At the time the Stein sisters arrived, there were about 1200 people in the camp; no less than 15 religious orders of men and women were represented among them. Each day the religious, clad in their habits, gathered to recite the Rosary and Office. In this holy assembly Edith stood out. An eyewitness who survived the horror recounted: ''She was sad, but not anxious. She gave the impression that the measure of suffering was so great that even when she smiled you were more afflicted.'' Part of the intense suffering of the people rested on the vague hope that the Nazis intended only to terrorize the Dutch bishops. Rumors abounded among the captives. Some felt sure they would eventually return home.

The eyewitness continued: ''I am sure Edith was thinking of the misery that she foresaw for the people, not her own. Her outward appearance gave me another thought: I remember her in the barracks—a Pieta without Christ.''

Another woman recalled that Sister Benedicta ''amazed all of us by her quietness and calm.'' The misery in the camp was indescribable.

''Sister Benedicta'' the lady remembered, ''moved about the women, quieting, helping and giving consolation. Many mothers, almost crazed themselves, were brooding in desperation. Sister Benedicta cared for them, washed and comforted them, and somehow provided food.''

After three days, the dreaded news spread about the camp: ''No one will be dismissed. All will be shipped to the East.''

Two men who had known the Stein sisters at Echt journeyed to Westerbork with food and blankets provided by the Jewish community. Dutch policemen arranged their entrance through the camp gates.

Later the visitors reported: ''We saw Sister Benedicta in her brown habit and black veil, in the company of Rosa. Our meeting was at the same time touching, sad and happy. They shook hands with us and for the first few moments we were mute.''

But so moved were all the participants that ''soon the words came.''

Edith's sister Rosa also became a Catholic. Both sisters died at Auschwitz.

The men gave the blankets and food to Sister Benedicta. She was thankful to the Jewish community, especially for their concern for Jews who had become Catholics. She told the visitors she was glad that some priests and nuns were among the people going to the camps, because "we are the only consolation for them."

"She said all this very quietly," the men noted. "Her eyes were beautiful, shining with the light of a holy Carmelite," the men remembered. She spoke to the Dutchmen about the repulsiveness of the camp, but never mentioned her own adversities.

"Her face created an atmosphere of heavenly life around her," the witnesses averred. "Several times she assured us that the Mother Prioress could be quite at peace about her and her sister." The men said, " 'Truly, very much at peace,' were the words she used."

One of the men offered a few words of compassion, to which Edith responded, "Whatever may happen to Rosa and me, we are ready; Christ is with us even here." Rosa and Edith shook hands with the men and wished them and their families God's blessing. The men turned away in tears.

A Dutch employee at the camp remembered Edith as "a truly great woman. In the hell of Westerbork, she lived only a few days, walking among the prisoners, talking to them and praying like a saint. Yes, that is what she was." The man, incensed that she was being treated so cruelly, offered to contact Dutch authorities and attempt to arrange her freedom. She was, in his eyes, no longer a Jew. "No, no. Don't, please," Edith responded. "Why should I be an exception? Everyone else in this group is going. It is good that we cannot profit from the fact that we were baptized. If I were exempted from the fate of the others, my life would be destroyed forever."

The employee remembered that she walked steadily and firmly to the railroad train that would carry her to Auschwitz. "I saw her smile. Her firmness was unbroken," he said.

On August 7, 1942, Edith, Rosa and their companions left Westerbork for Auschwitz. Two days later they were stripped, forced into line and marched into the gas chambers. Edith Stein, Sister Teresa Benedicta of the Cross, the relentless pursuer of truth, fully possessed—at last—him who said, "I am truth—I am life."

Charles de Foucauld

It is rare in human history for a bank to set a plaque on its walls honoring a man who died without a penny. But a bank in Strasbourg, France, has a plaque which reads: "Charles de Foucauld was born here September 15, 1858. He was an officer of the French cavalry, an explorer of Morocco, and a missionary. He was assassinated in North Africa on the first of December, 1916."

What is the reason for the plaque? Who was Charles de Foucauld? Why is his birthplace worth marking?

*   *   *   *   *

Charles was born into an aristocratic French family. His father, Francois Edouard, Vicomte de Foucauld, was deputy inspector of water and forests for the French government. His family had long enjoyed the confidence of both the French crown and French democratic governments. Charles could trace the de Foucauld roots back to the 10th century. The family had numbered among its members many heroes of both the faith and

63

the nation. Down the centuries the de Foucaulds had borne themselves bravely; they had lived up to their motto, "Never retreat." Charles' great-uncle, murdered during the French Revolution for refusing to collaborate with the godless revolutionaries, is a beatified martyr of the Catholic faith.

Charles' earliest memory was of a prayer taught him by his mother, Elisabeth de Morlet. "God bless Papa, Mama, Grandpapa, Grandmama, Grandmama de Foucauld, and my little sister," the prayer stated. Charles' little sister, Marie Ines, was born in 1861. Charles' home was an ideal one. Both children, Charles and Marie, were surrounded by the best that French culture could provide and all of this in an atmosphere of love, delight and joy. But such a happy condition was not to last. Late in the summer of 1863 Charles' father contracted tuberculosis. Unable to continue his work, in low spirits, and not wanting to infect his young children, Edouard went to Paris. The mother remained in Strasbourg with the children. In March of the following year, 1864, Charles' mother died as a result of a miscarriage. Charles remembered well his mother's last words: "Thy will, not mine, be done." In August 1864 Edouard died in Paris. Charles was not yet 6 and Marie less than 3.

"I was left an orphan very young," he wrote later on. Yet Charles did not think of his childhood as a time without joy. Indeed it was a time of deep joy for him, and the recollection of this joy, not the lack of it, enriched his memories as his life went on. His shattering childhood ex-

Charles with his mother, Elizabeth, and younger sister, Marie Ines.

perience of losing his parents left one deep effect upon him. Throughout his life, with all its ups and downs, he always remained protective and compassionate toward children, the helpless, the afflicted.

Their parents dead, Charles and Marie remained at Strasbourg in the home of their grandfather, Colonel de Morlet. De Morlet, tenderhearted and deeply attached to his grandchildren, probably spoiled Charles and his sister. If such was the case, it was only because the man wanted to fill as far as possible the gap left in the children's lives by the loss of their parents. Colonel de Morlet did his best, and Charles grew to be a warm, outgoing person who gave himself to the service of others. The colonel, in bestowing affection upon his grandson, built up his self-confidence, thus enabling Charles, in his turn, not only to feel affection but to show it.

Colonel de Morlet, a deeply loving man, imparted a capacity for kindness and generosity to Charles. He did this by fostering devotion to the family, country and God. Colonel de Morlet not only trained Charles in these ways but also gave him a taste for reading and serious study.

Besides the intellectual discipline and training, his grandfather inculcated a love for silence in young de Foucauld. To the very end of his life Charles remembered the woods around Saverne where he used to walk with his grandfather. The two would walk in silence, the stillness of the forest broken only by the whistle and warbling of the birds, the murmur of the insects.

Colonel de Morlet, Charles'
grandfather, raised his
grandchildren after their parents'
deaths.

Once more, cruel events disrupted the idyllic existence of Charles' early years. In 1870 the Franco-Prussian War cast its shadow over the de Foucauld family. During the course of that war the city of Strasbourg fell to the Prussian invaders. Then Paris fell and the French throne collapsed. As part of the conditions for peace, France had to cede the city of Strasbourg to Germany. Charles' grandfather, an ardent patriot and a former officer of the French army, had no choice in his heart other than to leave Strasbourg and to remain exiled for the rest of his days from the city he loved so much and regarded as his home.

Colonel de Morlet moved to Nancy in Lorraine, a beautiful city expressive of all the gentility and beauty of French culture. In Nancy, Charles began his education in earnest. He soon showed himself not only a normal young man but an extremely intelligent student. He entered the local high school at 13. As was the custom of the time, in his 14th year he made his first communion in the cathedral at Nancy. In a letter written to a cousin some 25 years after this day, Charles recalled it as "one of unclouded joy." He had been given long and careful preparation for first communion. His faith had been fostered by a loving Christian family. The example set so deeply into Charles' life by his grandfather was particularly effective. On this day of his first communion those who were dearest to Charles in the world were with him.

Yet, despite all the advantages that Charles had, as he grew into young manhood he lost his faith.

There is no doubt that the loss of faith was no sudden happening but, rather, a gradual process which found its roots in Charles' high school reading habits. He had become familiar with the irreligious and skeptical writers of his time. These French intellectuals created a climate of doubt about the basic tenets of religion. Many of these authors did not deny the existence of God, but they did proclaim humanity's inability to attain a certain knowledge of God's existence.

Thus Charles outgrew religion as presented to him in his childhood. He found nothing to take the place of the faith he rejected. It was not a comfortable situation for him since Charles could not stand being neutral about anything. In temperament he was a man who had to be committed to something, yet he could not be committed if his intellect was unsatisfied. This seemed to be the case as far as his Catholic faith was concerned. His

A high-school student, Charles is second from the left.

predicament was the kind experienced before and since by young people of intelligence, whose questioning minds are in search of belief.

*   *   *   *   *

Charles could not seem to find a goal or meaning for his life. Moved, perhaps, by the long tradition of the de Foucauld family, he decided to enter military service. He spent three years preparing for entrance into the military service of Saint-Cyr. So well did Charles prepare that he was 82nd out of 412 candidates in the entrance examination to the famous institution. But if Charles was intellectually distinguished, there was little else to distinguish him. A photograph at this time reveals him to be overweight and not particularly handsome. Indeed, the Saint-Cyr authorities almost rejected him for being overweight.

Saint-Cyr, southwest of Versailles, was a military school with a long and famous tradition. Its students, drawn mainly from France's distinguished families, felt called upon to carry on the great tradition of France's military glory. Learning strict obedience so that they could eventually command, these young Frenchmen gave themselves wholeheartedly to their military training. They wished to devote themselves as servants of France and, if need be, to die for their country.

To the end of Charles' strange, colorful life, Saint-Cyr left its imprint. While being much else besides, Charles remained the soldier and patriot, intense in his devotion to his beloved native France. At Saint-Cyr Charles continued to develop himself intellectually. He scored well in his military studies and manifested a genuine talent for the study of the classical Latin and Greek authors.

Charles finished his first year at Saint-Cyr with a very fine record. His superiors commended him on all counts.

The following February Charles was summoned from Saint-Cyr to Nancy. His beloved grandfather, Colonel de Morlet, was seriously ill. The old soldier died February 3, 1878, at the age of 81. Charles was 19. The grandfather had loved Charles with a deep and intense affection; the young man had returned that love.

The death of his grandfather seemed to be a summation of all the sorrows, the uncertainties, the upheavals that Charles had suffered in his life. After his grandfather's death Charles grew desperately unhappy. It seemed to this deeply affectionate young man that all the love and happiness he had known had gone out of his life.

His sadness and unhappiness were reflected in his lack of interest in his soldiering and his training. He became indifferent toward the military life that had made him so happy in his previous year at Saint-Cyr. His room was untidy; his bed badly made. He was late for his lectures. He forgot his books. His hair grew too long and his whole appearance became slovenly. All this brought down the heavy hand of his superiors. The former sharply turned out and mentally alert and disciplined cadet was becoming a disappointment.

In his despair Charles sought relief in the joys of food. Fellow officers referred to Charles at this time of his life as a gourmand. He caught the fancy of his fellow cadets by eating pate de foie gras (goose liver) with a silver spoon at night in the Saint-Cyr dormitory.

The upset and disoriented Charles now had a further complication added to his life. He inherited a large fortune from his grandfather.

Charles somehow managed to survive at Saint-Cyr amid all the turmoil of his life. He graduated from the military academy and received his commission as a sublieutenant in the French army. With this commission a new phase of his life began. He spent money lavishly and wildly. He gambled, drank and ate without restraint. He entertained on a grand scale. He was overweight and overdressed.

On one occasion Charles got into some trouble with the police, and the members of his aristocratic family expressed their anger and disgust at his unseemly conduct. One could hardly blame them; Charles was an aimless, purposeless, immature young man.

The displeasure of his family did not stop Charles from living up to all he felt was expected of a wealthy young lieutenant in the French army. He entered into an alliance with a young woman whom we know only as Mimi. Mimi brought Charles some comfort, and she enjoyed his company. She was not embarrassed by his wild conduct. So wild had this behavior become that the townspeople complained of the racket that constantly issued from his apartment and the type of people who visited him.

In his wild extravagance and near-riotous living, Charles was never known to be vicious. There are episodes of kindness that are somewhat touching, more so because they seem so out of character with his general lifestyle. For instance, if he saw someone losing at cards who could not afford to do so, he would contrive to lose in that person's place. He did this with such gentle grace that people would hardly notice. Despite his lack of faith and lack of discipline, Charles gradually began to manifest the kindness, generosity, friendliness and courage which became the hallmarks of his character in later life.

His regiment was ordered to Algeria, then a French colony. Charles dispatched Mimi ahead of him to prepare an apartment for them. When the regiment arrived and settled Charles insisted on parading Mimi in North Africa as the Vicomtesse de Foucauld. Again his aristocratic family reacted with wrath. The scandal, of course, reverberated into the headquarters of Charles' regiment, and his colonel asked him to get rid of Mimi. That the young officer had a mistress did not disturb the colonel all that much; that he paraded her as a member of the aristocratic de Foucaulds was too much for him to bear. So Charles was ordered to send Mimi home. He refused. Then his superiors ordered him back to France and charged him with a breach of discipline and notorious misconduct. He was found guilty of this charge and removed from active duty. Taking Mimi with him, he settled at Lake Geneva in Switzerland. They stayed at a hotel overlooking the beautiful lake.

Charles did not, however, fritter away his days at Geneva. He began to seriously study the North African dialects.

Charles' brief stay in North Africa had affected him deeply. That mysterious area of the world had cast a spell over him. It was the beginning of a love affair that would end only with his death.

One morning in May 1881, Charles opened his newspaper and read that his old regiment had been sent into action to quell a native revolt in Algeria. Charles immediately requested the military authorities to reinstate him and permit him to re-enlist in his regiment. He offered to rejoin the outfit as a private if that were the only way he could be accepted. The French authorities reinstated him as an officer and permitted him to rejoin his outfit. The price he had to pay was to break off his affair with Mimi. This he did, and nothing more was ever heard of Mimi.

With the cessation of the rebellion Charles requested his military superiors' permission to explore the vast and as yet little known territory of Morocco that adjoined Algeria in North Africa. When they refused him this permission, Charles resigned his commission and decided to undertake this very dangerous adventure on his own. In the eyes of his family Charles was up to another ne'er-do-well, harebrained scheme. He was indeed trying their patience. He had gone through an immense fortune; he had twice left the army; and now he was planning this dangerous and senseless enterprise. But Charles was able to win over most of his relatives, and they gradually accepted his decision. He made it clear to them that the purpose of this expedition was not merely to escape boredom through adventure but, rather, to make a scientific study of this unexplored territory.

He chose as his guide a Jewish rabbi named Mardochee, whose acquaintance Charles had made in Algiers, the capital of Algeria. Rabbi Mardochee was an experienced traveler and had a good reputation in French geographical circles.

To make the journey through Morocco Charles had to disguise

himself either as a Moslem or a Jew. The Moroccan natives would view a Christian and a Frenchman with deepest suspicion, not so much because of his religion but because he was European. European nations were at this time rapidly colonizing throughout Africa. So a Frenchman would be judged a spy.

He chose the disguise of a Jew because he felt he could travel largely ignored, unnoticed. Most Moroccans were Moslems, and few Moslems condescended to speak to Jews. This would leave Charles free to write notes and to use his meteorological instruments. He could, furthermore, conceal these instruments in the flowing garments worn by a Jewish rabbi.

*   *   *   *   *

At three o'clock on the afternoon of June 21, 1883, Charles de Foucauld made his first penetration of the Morocco territory. He traveled in a caravan with six or seven companions, most of them Jews, and about 10 baggage animals. Accompanying him was his guide, Rabbi Mardochee. The two of them, Mardochee and Charles, traveled this huge territory on foot during the ensuing months.

The bulk of Charles' scientific work was done under conditions that were most arduous and dangerous. Journeying from place to place, generally in the company of fellow travelers from whom he had to hide

Rabbi Mardochee, a Jewish geographer and scholar, guided Charles through Morocco's dangerous territory in 1883.

his identity, Charles made a practice of walking or riding ahead so as to be able to make notes unobserved by his traveling companions. In his right hand he carried a pencil that was only a stub; in his left a notebook, carefully concealed, not more than two inches square. "I was writing," he says, "all the time I was on the road." His flowing garments served to screen the movements of his hands as well as the compass with which he noted changes of direction and the barometer which enabled him to record the rise and fall of the ground. Working in this way he filled numerous small notebooks. Sometimes he devoted an entire night to recording the findings of the day, transferring them from the smaller notebooks into a larger book.

Charles published the results of his journey in a document called *The Reconnaissance of Morocco*. The work won worldwide acclaim in scientific circles.

If it was true that Charles had discovered many things about Morocco, so was it true that Morocco and its inhabitants led Charles to discover many things about himself. Throughout the year in the desert Charles came into contact with no Christians. He encountered only Moslems and Jews. He had lost his Christian faith some years earlier, or so he had concluded. But during the Morocco exploration something stirred within Charles. The stirrings were prompted partly by his encounter with the Jews. He could not help but envy their belief in their God, a belief which survived all kinds of suffering and persecution. Their faith certainly did not provide the Jews with any great material comfort. Yet their belief was as strong or even stronger than death itself. This fact made Charles think.

The simple and direct faith of the Moslems also affected him deeply. Rough, hard, tough desert people, the Moslems believed in their God with all their heart. God was as real to them as the desert and mountains of Morocco in which they lived.

More than once, when traveling with these little groups of Moslems, Charles would observe them five times each day kneeling and facing toward Mecca to pray. So overwhelming was the effect of the Moslems and their attitude of faith upon Charles that for a time he actually thought of adopting their religion.

Yet, much as he was impressed by Judaism and Islam, there were times in Morocco when he hankered after the Christianity in which he no longer believed. Charles' life was not enviable. His rejection of the Christian faith brought him no sense of liberation but rather a feeling of frustration and despair.

"I have despaired of finding truth," he wrote at this time. He had not actually abjured his faith and denied the existence of God; he simply found no meaning in his former beliefs. And so, while the Morocco expedition indicated that exteriorly Charles had made great strides in his life, interiorly he was in turmoil. The self-indulgent young man who had once brought disgrace upon his family had now proved himself by his journey to Morocco. Acclaimed both for his courage and his intellectual and scientific achievements, he had honored the name of de Foucauld. Yet there was an emptiness within him he could not seem to handle.

He considered marriage and actually was engaged to a young French noblewoman, Mademoiselle Titre. He loved her dearly, yet he broke off the engagement. He felt he was not ready for marriage and would only complicate her life the more by entering it. Full of unrest, disappointed, bewildered, Charles seemed to have reached a dead end. Yet it was at precisely this point that the grace of God entered his life in a dramatic way to help him discover the meaning of his life and to begin the work of the great vocation God had in store for him.

In a side chapel of St. Augustine's Church in Paris there is another plaque marking the career of Charles de Foucauld. It reads: "Here Charles Foucauld returned to God in the confession he made to Abbe Huvelin in October, 1886. [Many years] Later at this same place, as a priest, he often celebrated holy Mass."

Returning to Paris after breaking his engagement to Mademoiselle Titre, Charles again found his life empty. Not quite knowing why, he began going each day to St. Augustine's Church, kneeling long hours, and repeating what he later called his "strange prayer": "My God, if you exist, make your presence known to me."

During this painful and confusing time, Charles' cousin Marie de Bondy proved a support and strength for him. "One person," he wrote, "who by her silence, her gentleness, her goodness, and deep intelligence sustained, strengthened and guided me at this time." Charles greatly admired Marie's qualities which were combined with a profound intelligence. It occurred to Charles that Marie's faith was a matter of deepest conviction for her. He then began to conclude that faith could not be the empty, vapid thing he thought it was if a woman of her character and intelligence could hold it with such profound conviction.

He confronted Marie with this thinking, and she suggested to him that he bring the problem of his faith to Abbe Huvelin. Abbe Huvelin's dialogue and discussion, his immense patience, and his profound insight into Charles' mind and heart, guided the Vicomte de Foucauld to return to his faith.

Until his death in 1910, the Abbe remained Charles' spiritual guide and director. But, most important, he guided Charles during the immediate aftermath of his conversion. With characteristic impetuosity, Charles at once decided that he wanted to be a religious and a monk. Abbe Huvelin would have none of it. He made Charles wait two years. The Christ of the gospels was the model ever present in de Foucauld's mind.

Charles sensed that he wanted to live as nearly as possible the hidden life of Jesus of Nazareth. In August 1888, Marie de Bondy again helped Charles take a serious step in the formation of his vocation. She brought him to visit the Trappist monastery at Fontgombault. The visit made a lasting impression on Charles. The sight of the monks in their humble, quiet lives and the poverty of their shabby, torn habits fired Charles' imagination. "This poverty," Madame de Bondy later wrote, "won his heart."

During the winter of 1888, Charles, at the request of Abbe

Marie de Bondy, Charles' cousin, helped him in the formation of his vocation.

Huvelin, made a pilgrimage to the Holy Land. Nazareth made a tremendous impact on him. The peace and tranquillity of the town moved him as few things in his whole life had. It confirmed him in his desire to become a religious. Following consultation with Abbe Huvelin and Madame de Bondy, Charles made his decision. He wrote his sister and informed her that he was going to enter the Trappist monastery of Our Lady of the Snows in Ardeche, France.

From the very beginning of his Trappist life, Charles desired to imitate the holiness of the Christ. Although untrained for it, he accepted manual work with great love and joy.

Physical labor was a source of consolation to him because it resembled the work of our Lord. He impressed his fellow monks as a man of unusual devotion, one who was extreme in his practice of austerities. But, in recalling his career among them, fellow Trappists remembered that Charles had good judgment and got along very well with others. Charles had taken the name Brother Alberic, and the monks remembered him as a man who "never refused to do anything for anyone."

Eventually Charles transferred to another Trappist monastery in the Near East in the wilds of Syria, at Akbes. The monks here lived even more poorly than the monks in France. They put in long, hard days at work and ate very little. They maintained, of course, the Trappist silence.

But Charles simply could not find the littleness of Christ of Nazareth in the Trappist monastery. Since he could not find what his heart

Abbe Huvelin was Charles' spiritual guide and director from the time of Charles' conversion until the Abbe's death.

sought in this most rigorous of Catholic religious orders, Charles had to search elsewhere. There existed no institution in which he could live in accordance with the mystery of Nazareth as he interpreted it, so the question came to him, "Why not found an order yourself?" Charles felt that the church needed such a religious order. So, from this point on, Charles struggled with two aspects of his life that became inseparable and which defined his life work more clearly. One, his personal vocation to live the hidden life of the Christ of Nazareth; and, two, his plans for establishing a new religious order in the church whose members would live in the manner of the Christ of Nazareth.

As this vocation became clearer and clearer to Charles, he determined to make his move. With proper permissions from his superiors, Charles left the Trappists and began a new chapter in his life.

* * * * *

Mother St. Michael was the Abbess of the Franciscan Poor Clares at Nazareth where Charles was engaged as a gardener and sacristan.

When Charles left the Trappists, various people had different opinions, both kind and unkind, about his departure. His friend Abbe Huvelin was puzzled by it all, but he recognized that Charles could no longer remain a Trappist. "It was impossible for him," the Abbe later stated. If Charles wanted literally to follow the hidden life of Christ of Nazareth, it occurred to the Abbe that the best place for him was Nazareth itself. So Abbe Huvelin advised Charles to attach himself as a porter and handyman to some religious house in Nazareth, possibly a Franciscan monastery where he could live at the door, alone, independent and not subject to the Franciscan rule. Charles arrived at the Monastery of the Franciscan Poor Clares at Nazareth on March 5, 1897, and the abbess, Mother St. Michael, engaged him as a man of all work. Charles lived in a garden of the monastery in a tall, narrow hut, rather like a sentry box. His work was not exacting, and he had plenty of opportunity to live in the spirit of the littleness he so desired. He swept, went on errands, gardened, served Mass and benediction, acted as sacristan. The remaining time he spent in prayer, meditation and reading. A fairly good artist, he painted pictures for the nuns, including meticulous black-and-white drawings of Nazareth that survive to the present.

Happy in this new life, Charles wrote, "My life here is what I have dreamed of so many years." He wrote Abbe Huvelin that he felt that "in his days of work and nights of prayer he had found what he had longed for" since the time of his confession and conversion. Clearly God had prepared a place for him in Nazareth. Abbe Huvelin wrote that he was happy that Charles had chosen to remain at Nazareth, in the shadow of St. Francis.

Charles also worked at the Poor Clare monastery in Jerusalem. Here he met Mother Elisabeth, the abbess. Charles had heard about the slaughter of Christians in Armenia and of the thousands who had died without priestly care. Mother Elisabeth pointed out that had a priest been there he could have helped those people. Charles began to see that it did not necessarily follow that if he became a priest he would have to leave the life of littleness he so desired. With Mother Elisabeth's help he realized that in the priestly vocation he could grow in the spirit of humility and abnegation and at the same time be able to bring Christ in the Mass and the sacraments to others.

As he thought more and more about the priesthood he continued to remain irrepressible in his desire to establish a new religious order.

These ideas came to light in Charles' somewhat confused correspondence with Abbe Huvelin. Not yet convinced beyond the shadow of a doubt that acceptance of the priesthood would not gradually erode his desire for littleness, Charles in his letters at this time revealed the indecision that he suffered. It is a measure of the Abbe's great love and admiration for Charles that he patiently guided him toward making the final decision to become a priest. Eventually the matter was settled. Charles returned to France and was ordained a priest.

*   *   *   *   *

Charles intended to return to the Holy Land after his ordination and to take up the same hidden and simple life that he had pursued at Nazareth. It occurred to him, however, that the hidden life of Nazareth could be lived anywhere. His thoughts increasingly turned to his first love, North Africa, and particularly to the Sahara region which had impressed him so deeply. In the Holy Land, he reflected, there were more than enough priests. In the vast area which he had explored in Morocco there were no priests. He remembered the kindness and generosity the desert Moslems so often showed him during his explorations. It was to these people he wanted to go, as well as to the French soldiers garrisoned in the Sahara. During his army days he had seen fellow soldiers die with no priest to administer to them.

In a letter to a friend at this time Charles described how his vocation was beginning to become crystal-clear. He wished to combine silence and service. "The silence of the cloister is not the silence of forgetfulness," he wrote. He did not wish to establish in Morocco a large monastery but, in accordance with his thinking about a new religious order, a rather lowly hermitage where a few monks could live on some barley harvested by their own hands. This little community would practice universal charity, sharing the little they had with whoever should come, guest or stranger. They would receive every human being who knocked at their door, whether traveler or soldier, whether Christian, Moslem, Jew or pagan. He hoped to establish a little center of prayer and hospitality.

This idea of a center of prayer and hospitality was not unknown among the Moslems. Throughout Morocco Charles had encountered these little places of prayer and hospitality where travelers could go and be cared for.

His mind made up, he sailed for Algiers on September 6, 1901. In October he set out for Beni-Abbes, a tiny settlement at the edge of the Moroccan desert. Here he established his first little center of prayer and hospitality. Father Charles constructed his tiny hermitage of mud bricks and palm trunks. The structure contained a chapel and sacristy, a guest room, and three tiny rooms for the companion monks whom Charles hoped would soon come to join him. The fact that he had no companions at this time did not discourage him at all. Charles, it seems, was ever the optimist.

To Marie de Bondy he described the purpose of his life at Beni-Abbes, "I want to accustom everyone here—Christian, Moslem, Jew, pagan—to look on me as a brother to each one of them." Charles loved the physical surroundings of Beni-Abbes, and they were indeed symbolic of the limitless range of the vocation to which God had called him.

Constructing a timetable for each day, he divided the hours among prayer, meditation, reading, theological studies, and manual work. The peace, solitude and hidden life that Charles had so long desired were within his grasp. But, as things turned out, his neat, highly organized day was never really his own. Constantly interrupted by visitors, French soldiers, desert travelers, slaves and the poor, Charles watched his view of his vocation slip through his fingers like the sand of the desert. In January 1902, he wrote:

I am astonished to see myself passing from the contemplative life to the life of the sacred ministry. Every day there are guests for supper, people seeking lodging. There

Paul Embarek and Abdiesus, both of whom Charles purchased from slavery, are pictured with him at Beni-Abbes.

> are guests for breakfast. It never stops. Sometimes I have up to eleven guests in one night. I often have between sixty and a hundred visitors in a day.

People soon came to call the little hermitage he had constructed "the Fraternity." The Fraternity had grown into a hive of activity. With warm hospitality Charles welcomed everyone who came. A visitor shared whatever Charles had by way of food. Having the full spirit of Christ himself, he gave that spirit of joy and brotherhood to all who came to him. His own food was meager and sometimes he lived on bread and water alone. He was happy in his role of servant and brother to all.

Among the guests Charles treated most tenderly were the slaves. During the early part of the century, slavery flourished in Morocco. Charles never encouraged the slaves to revolt or even to attempt escape. Either course would have had little chance of success and would result only in more suffering for these unfortunates. On several occasions Charles protested vigorously to the French authorities. He regarded slavery as unjust and immoral and felt that it was the French government's duty to put an end to this despicable practice once and for all. Ceaselessly Charles put pressure on government and ecclesiastical authorities to wipe out the institution of slavery in Morocco. His efforts, however, came to naught. He himself did what he could by redeeming slaves with what little money he had or could beg from friends and family for that express purpose.

Thus Charles' time at Beni-Abbes passed rapidly and productively. For him it was a time of intense joy and peace and a time full of surprises. Not the least surprise came from an old Saint-Cyr comrade, now a general in the French Army, Henri Laperrine. Laperrine invited Charles to come to a section of Algeria called the Hoggar, which was under his jurisdiction. The Tuareg tribes lived in this section of North Africa. Charles, interested in Laperrine's offer, was torn between remaining at Beni-Abbes and undertaking this mission to the Tuareg. After correspondence with Abbe Huvelin, he decided to journey to the Tuareg.

Charles visited these tribes with his characteristic energy and complete devotion. He studied the Tuareg language, as he described, "with all my might." And he determined right away to translate the four gospels into Tuareg. He undertook the journey to win the confidence of the Tuareg and to establish peace. To achieve these ends he gave himself completely to the tribesmen. He provided them with what little medicines he had, gave them alms, and offered them hospitality no matter where he was.

At the basis of this activity was Charles' genuine respect for the Tuareg. He wished to show himself their brother. "We are all brothers," he wrote. "We hope to be all one day in the same Heaven, and we all hope to pray for one another." He describes the purpose of his life at this time, "to pray with all my heart for the Tuareg: that is my life."

During his missionary journey through the Tuareg region, Charles lived as a nomad, going from place to place. He permitted himself no rest. In one location he constructed a makeshift chapel out of branches. And he placed on top of this a wooden cross. Inside this chapel Charles set up an altar and covered it with a tent to protect it from the dust. He wrote a prayer for the occasion: "Sacred Heart of Jesus, thank you for this first tabernacle in the Tuareg country. May it be the first of many." He desired to show that the Christian religion "was all charity, all love; its emblem, a heart."

Despite his constant movement through the Tuareg country, Charles continued his studies of the Tuareg language and actually completed his translation of the four gospels.

Two principles which later guided Charles' work among the Tuareg emerged from his first experience with them. First, he realized that if he was to live among them his life had to be simple because their lives were simple. He would have to live in great poverty. Second, his old dream of followers to continue his work was revived. He visualized once more small groups of Christians living among the Tuareg. These groups would consist of women as well as men. He knew that the Tuareg women, as free as European women, would respond to the Christian message.

After much prayer and soul-searching, and seeking advice from Marie de Bondy and Abbe Huvelin, Charles decided in May 1905 to leave Beni-Abbes and re-enter the Hoggar to work among the Tuareg on a more permanent basis. Returning to the Hoggar, he searched for a location to establish a small hermitage similar to the one in Beni-Abbes. Four months passed before Charles found a suitable place. All during this journey Charles gave much time to any person he met who requested it. He dedicated part of every day, even during these journeys, to continuing his study of the Tuareg language. Finally, in August 1905, he arrived at the place that won his heart. It was called Tamanrasset. He wrote:

> I chose Tamanrasset, a village of twenty homes, right in the
> mountains, in the heart of the Hoggar, far from all important
> centers. I do not think there is ever likely to be a garrison,
> telegraph or a European here; it will be long before there is
> any type of European activity or mission here. I chose this
> abandoned place and here I remain.

Accompanying the French priest during the journey from Beni-Abbes to
Tamanrasset was a young man called Paul, whom Charles had purchased
from slavery. Immediately Charles and Paul set to work to build a little hut
and chapel and to provide a place of hospitality for the travelers Charles
knew would not be long in coming. Charles seemed to have no fear about living in the midst of Moslems. Even though as a European he might be in
danger, Charles was convinced his life was in God's hands.

In September he offered his first Mass at Tamanrasset. He wrote:

> I congratulate myself for being in this country and in this par-
> ticular spot. There are very few permanent inhabitants, but
> there are many nomads in the vicinity. The nomads and some
> of the settled inhabitants are already in the habit of coming to
> me to ask for needles and medicine. The poor occasionally
> ask for a little grain.

Father de Foucauld's little home was quickly becoming a center of
love.

Along with this work of charity, Charles was preparing a Tuareg-
French and French-Tuareg dictionary. This work was very important to him
since it was another example of his basic respect for the Tuareg people.
Charles wished not only to establish verbal communication with them but
also hoped that by better understanding of their language and their poetry he
could come to a deeper love and appreciation of the Tuareg. He wrote:

> I had to gain the confidence of the Tuareg, make friends with
> them, do them small services, give them useful advice, tact-
> fully encourage them to follow natural religion, show them
> that we Christians love them. That is all that can be done for
> most of them here, at Beni-Abbes, or elsewhere. If I meet
> with somebody who is especially well-disposed, I can go a bit
> further.

His deep regard for the Tuareg did not blind him to their faults. But he saw them as a people of gentle character, who were always laughing and joking. Unlike other Moslems, they were monogamous. Thus Charles concluded that they must have been Christians before the Islam conquest. They were also attached to the symbol of the cross, and this confirmed Charles' suspicion that at one time this tribe had been Christian.

Father de Foucauld was acutely aware of the role Christian women could play in bettering conditions among the Tuareg. Women were needed, he stated, "who would make themselves loved and blessed, not only for the practical services they could render, but for the influence they could wield among a people who were proud of their descent from a queen."

But neither men nor women came to follow Charles. At the end of 1906 he thought a long-awaited companion might join him. A young man did come and attempted to live Charles' form of life. The candidate remained only a few months with Charles, then abandoned the adventure as too rough for him. Charles never attracted another vocation for the rest of his days on earth.

After establishing the little center at Tamanrasset, Charles decided to move into the neighboring regions and make contact with other Tuareg people. He also wished during this journey to gather more material for his work on the Tuareg poetry. A Negro guide who had an endless memory for Tuareg verses accompanied Charles on this venture. Charles would encourage his

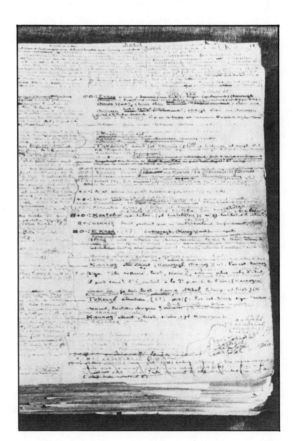

Charles spent countless hours preparing a Tuareg-French dictionary to help him better understand and appreciate the Tuareg people.

memory by paying him a *sou* for every Tuareg verse he recited. During the journey the French priest would also sit by the hour under a tree or in a tent writing down verses recited by women and children whom he had encountered on the journey. The results of much of this effort is evident in two fine volumes of Tuareg verse which were published under Charles de Foucauld's name after his death.

The Tuareg verse books are scholarly and meticulous and provide translations from the Tuareg into French which are marvels of lucidity. De Foucauld fittingly and lovingly invoked the Tuareg world. It was easy to see Charles' loving attitude toward these people reflected in his translating work. He accepted the Tuareg as his equals and never patronized or displayed unwanted superiority over them. He believed they were his brothers and sisters, and he lived by that principle.

Charles eventually returned to Tamanrasset, and he was delighted with the welcome the people there gave him. Tamanrasset was suffering a dreadful drought when he returned. He wrote: "The goats are as dry as the soil, the inhabitants nearly as dry as the goats." Somehow Charles managed to provide a free meal every day for the children. He was happy to see them, as he said, "chewing away." He went short of food himself. Charles always loved children. His own nephews and nieces were objects of his great affection and generosity. At Beni-Abbes as many as 60 children came to see him in a day. The young, completely at ease with Charles, could laugh and joke with him without fearing to give any offense. He shared their problems and sometimes sought pardon on their behalf from outraged elders. Occasionally he intervened in unhappy family situations which could have ended in tragedy but which, because of his care, ended in happy reconciliation.

In January 1908 Charles fell ill. He was panting, he wrote, "like an old camp horse"; he was unable to eat or even to sleep. He had fainting spells. So distressed was he that he wrote to his friend General Laperrine, asking for condensed milk, a little wine, and some other things to get him back on his feet. He confessed later: "My letter to General Laperrine was not at all what a letter from a man of self-denial should be." The general sent all that Charles requested and added three camels laden with other provisions. Laperrine himself came to Tamanrasset to visit his friend. There, in general-like fashion, he remonstrated with Charles because of the severe penances.

Laperrine also wrote to Father de Foucauld's ecclesiastical superiors and explained that Charles' illness was brought on because the priest had gone short of food to provide for the children who suffered during the drought.

What contributed most to Charles' eventual recovery, besides the food and medicine provided by General Laperrine, was the touching concern the Tuareg people manifested for him. Despite the drought they searched over the wide and wild territory of the Hoggar to find goats that had milk so that they could provide this comfort for Charles.

Charles never shared the view held by many that Moslems could not eventually embrace Christianity. Christ, he felt, had come to all peoples without distinction. But de Foucauld did not feel that preaching was the way to bring Christ to the Moslems. They were a stubborn people. He felt that preaching, instead of bringing them closer to Christ, would only make them defiant and harder to reach. He saw his task and the task of his successors as that of being patient and prudent; to make friends, remove prejudice, build up confidence. He felt that knowledge of the religious truths of Christianity, while it had to be communicated to the world, could only be spread very slowly. "Centuries," he wrote, "must pass between the spadework and the final harvest, but this is no reason for apathy and discouragement." He looked upon his immediate task as that of opening doors. He felt he could open the main door by accepting the Tuareg with respect, as his equals before God.

He said with confidence that he was doing good at Tamanrasset. He wrote, "Knowing that I am always on the spot, people come to see me, for they are sure of finding me." The reasons for the coming of the Tuareg were many. Tribal leaders often came to discuss affairs of the Hoggar and the future of the people. Women came to take advantage of the little gifts that cousin Marie de Bondy often sent from Paris. They particularly loved the black dye to hide their graying hairs!

Between Christmas of 1908 and March 1909, Charles visited France. During his stay there he had the opportunity of renewing his contacts with Marie de Bondy, his cousin, and Abbe Huvelin, his spiritual guide. He also established an association of lay people whose members were to live by the gospel. He wished members of this association to read and reread the gospels so that they would be filled with the spirit of Christ. He felt that these people could become apostles, not so much by means of external activity, but by the

Charles and Ouksem, a Tuareg prince, visit with Marie de Bondy and her husband on a trip to France.

goodness of their lives, their warmth and affection toward others. While in France he sought recruits for this new association and did gather some.

Returning to Tamanrasset in June, he found the country in a better state than when he had departed. There had been rain, the first in three and a half years. The dolls he brought with him from France caused great excitement among the Tuareg. He wrote to his cousin Marie: "There is no one, big or small, who does not ask to see the dolls." He returned in a mood of optimism, almost elation—more than ever determined not to be held back by difficulties.

He seemed to accept now that difficulties were not a passing state, not a gale that would eventually blow itself out, but rather the normal condition of life. Impatient by temperament, he sought to school himself in patience. He was very fond of St. Teresa of Avila's favorite prayer:

> Be thou by naught perturbed,
> Of naught be afraid,
> For all things pass
> Save God,
> Who does not change.
> Be patient, and at last
> Thou shalt of all
> Fulfillment find.
> Hold God,
> And naught shall fail thee,
> For he alone is All.

For Charles the days passed at Tamanrasset in a quiet life of service. Devoting himself completely to the people about him and continuing his intellectual labors, he found a great deal of peace and joy. A French visitor to Tamanrasset wrote of this stage in Charles' career:

> His hermitage has to be seen to be believed. Imagine a room forty-five feet long; that is Father Foucauld's dwelling, a passage. Inside, a prodigious quantity of things, books, boxes, etc., crammed onto homemade bookcases. Yet all is in perfect order. I can't understand how so many things can fit into so small a space and still leave room for someone to live there. You can't in fact walk two abreast, however thin you may be.

On August 31, 1914, Charles de Foucauld reached page 550 of the

Tuareg-French dictionary he was preparing. A few days later he learned that war had broken out in Europe. On September 15, his 56th birthday, he wrote:

> I shall not leave Tamanrasset; my place is here, to help maintain calm among the people. The Tuareg have never even heard the name of Germany and know nothing of European affairs. They will carry on as usual, occupied only with the concerns of each day, without any idea of the hurricane sweeping over us, unless they are stirred up from Algeria, the Sudan, or Tripoli, or excited by rash words or orders from French officers or officials.

Late in 1914 Charles again fell ill. He ran a high temperature, suffered headaches, and experienced difficulty in breathing. A French doctor from a nearby military fort visited him and wrote: "Father Charles was suffering from scurvy and was in serious condition. I have seen this coming on for some time, for he leads the most unhealthy life imaginable."

By mid-January Charles had recovered his health. Tamanrasset seemed quiet, yet there was some tension in the quiet desert air.

A tribe from Tripoli called the Senoussistes had revolted against the Allied governments and attacked the French fort in the area near Charles. After the attack the Senoussistes remained a constant, if unseen, threat to the peace of Tamanrasset.

The following year the situation did not improve, and Charles was aware that he was in danger. In September 1916, he wrote to his cousin Marie:

> My life follows outwardly its customary calm, but I have an additional occupation lately. I have built an enclosure about forty-two feet square, with a well, which can serve as a refuge for the population here in case of a military attack. I have transported my hermitage here.

Despite his concern the winter of 1916 was passing quietly for Charles. December 1, 1916, was a particularly beautiful day. Charles wrote in his diary on that day:

> I do not think there is any danger to us from the Senoussistes. Our troops are strongly reinforced and will be able, I hope, to force the enemy back beyond the Moroccan frontier. The country is very quiet.

Charles was murdered at the "Fraternity" at Tamanrasset on December 1, 1916.

At 7:00 p.m. Paul, his companion, left the little hermitage and returned to his home. Charles was alone. His books and manuscripts were about him. Because he had been expecting a courier that day he was in the midst of some last-minute writing. Suddenly a loud knock at his door broke the silence. Charles went to the door and opened it. Rough hands seized him, dragged him outside, bound his elbows behind him, and flung him to his knees. It was the long-feared Senoussistes. The invaders left a 15-year-old boy, armed with a rifle, to keep guard over Father de Foucauld while they pillaged the homes of the nearby Tuareg in the little compound. While Charles was kneeling on the ground he happened to look up to see two French soldiers coming to visit him. They were completely unaware of the raid in progress. As they approached, Charles made a movement as if to warn them. The young guard, thinking Charles was trying to free himself, panicked. He put his hand to the trigger of his rifle and shot Father de Foucauld through the head. The bullet lodged in the wall of the hermitage at the right of the door. The hole is visible today.

Death had come out of the night, a violent death, yet not the martyr-dom which Charles at one time craved. Charles' death was befitting one who in life had sought the lowest place, a death dealt by the hand of a frightened boy. The invaders killed the two French soldiers after Charles' murder, and in the morning the Tuareg buried the three men together. Their graves were marked by a wooden cross, and military honors were paid to the victims.

The French captain in charge of the burial detail found sheets of manuscripts littering Charles' hermitage. Imbedded in the sand on the hermitage floor a small monstrance containing the sacred host was found. The captain took the monstrance, wrapped it in a handkerchief, placed it in front of him on the saddle of his mount, and carried it 30 miles to the nearest French fort. There he conferred with a noncommissioned officer, a former seminarian. Following this conference the captain donned a pair of white gloves, took the host from the monstrance, and the soldier, kneeling down, received it from him

*   *   *   *   *

Since his days in Nazareth, Charles de Foucauld had sensed that he would die a violent death. This became a strange consolation to him. He bore the disappointment of never attracting any followers by feeling that in death his life would make some sense to others and attract them to follow the path he had marked. He drew great strength from the words of Christ: "Unless the grain of wheat falls to the ground and dies, it remains alone. But if it dies, it bears much fruit." Indeed the scripture quotation could be an epitaph for Charles de Foucauld. When he died he had not one single follower. The association of Christian readers of the gospel that he had begun in France had attracted a mere handful, but only one person was an active member. Yet both the history of Charles de Foucauld and his spirituality have taken on new meaning and seem to be very attractive to people of our times.

The work of Father de Foucauld is attractive to the modern world because the French priest saw himself not so much as an evangelist but as a builder of foundations for eventual evangelization. He felt he could achieve this goal most effectively by eliminating the difficulties that missionaries who would succeed him would have to face. Thus his intense dedication to the study of the Tuareg language. He undertook this arduous labor not simply to learn words but to establish a bridge from his own heart into the very spirit and thought of the Tuareg people. Perhaps this work is a clue to the root of his genius—that is, his respect for every one of God's creatures. Contrary to so many of his contemporaries in both political and religious life, Charles saw each human being as a child of God and one who stood as his equal, regardless of color or creed, in the sight of God. In his view of reality all people throughout the whole world were truly brothers and sisters. There was no place in his thinking for racism, for slavery, for the subtle evil of patronizing. The spirit of compassion for all, particularly the poor, moved Charles de Foucauld to willingly face loneliness and isolation in Christ's service and to zealously spread the good news of the gospel to all cultures. This same spirit that moved him eventually attracted many followers to his way of life.

Five religious congregations in today's church draw their inspiration from his spirituality: the Little Brothers of Jesus, the Little Sisters of the Sacred Heart, the Little Sisters of Jesus, the Little Brothers and the Little Sisters of the Gospel. These groups, despite the turmoil in post-Vatican II religious life, continue to show a steady increase in candidates.

Various groups of priests and laity, men and women, married and single, who wish to live in accordance with the spiritual ideals set forth by Charles have developed throughout the world. The basic theme that unites all these groups can be expressed in one word: littleness. It was the littleness, the poverty and humility of the hidden Christ of Nazareth that Charles pursued all the days of his life. It is his heritage to those who, attracted by his spirit, have sought to search out its depths and meaning. Father Rene Voillaume, the present leader of the Little Brothers of Jesus, perhaps expressed it best: "Little we are and little we shall be in the eyes of men." This is the spirit that animated Charles de Foucauld. It is this spirit that guides those who are seeking to follow him in today's world.

The life of Charles de Foucauld leaves little doubt that he was a man who lived very close to God. In the face of his human frailties he ascended through the various stages of perfection to that point where he was regarded by those who knew him as an individual of a very saintly life. In 1927 the first steps were taken to introduce the cause of his beatification. In 1947 the documents were forwarded to Rome. Only time, the devotion of the people, and the definition of the church can tell that Charles of Jesus was indeed a saint.

Vincent Lebbe

It was 2 a.m. and he couldn't sleep. He tossed about in his bed, his wiry body vainly attempting to shake off the anger that boiled within him.

"They can't do this . . . they fooled me . . . they spoke out of both sides of their mouths. . . ."

"Fifteen years of my life. . . ." The remembrance of those years of dedicated priestly service as a missionary in China caused him to draw his knees up against his chest. Then, like a powerful spring uncoiling, he leaped out of bed and made for a small table in his room that served as his desk.

He lit a lamp. Lying beside the light was the note that had enraged him and his unfinished response.

Once more he read the note. It was from Paris, dated March 1917.

> You will leave your present post and report to mission head-quarters, Kashing. You will no longer function as Vicar General of Tientsin. Bishop Dumond has been so informed. Signed, Vicar General, Congregation of the Mission.

He shook his head and sat down to make yet one more effort to write his reply. But once again anger overcame him. Putting down his pen, he pushed his chair back and began to pace back and forth across the room. From time to time he clenched his fist and roared into the night.

The priest, a calm, pleasant man, generally faced life's trials with humor and verve. But now events had closed tightly about him. As a Vincentian he valued and had always conscientiously observed his vow of obedience. He felt that to accept the orders the note contained would be to destroy the great dream that had given shape and purpose to his missionary life. To be obedient now, he felt, was to cooperate with the very forces of ignorance and injustice that were, in his view, undermining the missionary effort of the Catholic church in China.

"O God," he prayed aloud, "what shall I do?"

*   *   *   *   *

Frederick's father, Fermin, was a Belgian lawyer with a keen sense of justice and integrity.

The question was one Father Lebbe rarely asked. From his boyhood, Freddy Lebbe had been decisive. His parents, Firmin Lebbe and Louise Barrier, had trained their sons and daughters to think clearly and independently. Freddy, their first-born son, exercised without hesitation the prerogatives and authority of his honored position over the other children. Firmin had married Louise while he was still studying law in Ghent, Belgium. Louise, a decently educated but penniless French-English governess, had taken employment with one of Firmin's aunts before she met her future husband. Firmin's father, a well-to-do, middle-class Belgian, was so angered by Firmin's choice of a girl of such modest financial circumstances that he cut off his son without a cent. Firmin and Louise somehow scraped up the money so the new husband could complete his education. The newlyweds had set up housekeeping in a garret in Ghent, and Frederic Lebbe was born there August 19, 1877. As his seven children arrived, one by one, Firmin progressed in the legal profession.

Although the Lebbes moved frequently between Belgium and France, they were united by a family atmosphere of affection and mutual respect that continued to develop irrespective of location. Wherever they were, in Paris or a Belgian provincial town, the Lebbes were at home with one another.

Religion was important to the family. Firmin had abandoned its practice as a young man, but returned to his Catholic faith before his marriage. Louise, raised a Protestant, became Catholic just before she met Firmin. During their years of marriage, both practiced their faith sincerely and devoutly. Neither appeared outwardly pious. Their generosity to the poor, their kindness and concern for each other and for their children, and their steady practice of prayer indicated the strength of their inner convictions. Firmin and Louise inculcated the same qualities in their offspring by their lives more than by their words.

Frederic made his first communion in Ypres, Belgium. Small and wiry, quick in movement and in mind, the boy had dark eyes that sparkled

His mother, Louise, was a clear-headed religious woman.

with intelligence and good humor and sometimes with anger. He had a hot temper that could blaze out on occasion.

Once he wrote a poem for a homework assignment which the teacher judged so beautifully written that he read it to the class. Freddy beamed with pride. When he collected his paper after class he noticed the teacher had written beside the poem, "This has been copied." Freddy exploded. Even in later life he would boil with anger when he recalled the incident.

As a young boy, Freddy came across a book about Blessed Jean Gabriel Perboyre, a Vincentian priest who suffered martyrdom in China in 1840. Blessed Jean's story so moved 11-year-old Freddy that he announced to all the family, "I am going to join the Vincentians, go to China, and become a martyr."

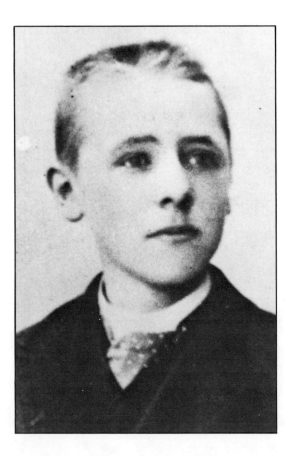

Only once did it seem he would not do this. As a teenager he fell head over heels in love. Whether the girl knew it or not, no one knows, but the whole Lebbe family knew it. There was so much trust and love among the Lebbes that Freddy was not ashamed to share his love pangs with his family.

Freddy survived the bout with Cupid and returned once more to his original desire.

*   *   *   *   *

"I am Vincent Lebbe." With these words 18-year-old Freddy introduced himself to the rector of the Vincentian Seminary of St. Lazare in

Frederick Lebbe as a young man of 15.

Paris in November 1895. The rector was so highly impressed that he didn't notice this new candidate, who had been baptized *Frederic* Lebbe, had suddenly become *Vincent* Lebbe.

There was always a method behind Freddy's madness. He loved and respected St. Vincent de Paul and wished to imitate the great French apostle of charity. Later, in the seminary, he wrote:

> Just as Vincent penetrated the world of his day, and adapted himself to its customs, ideas and manners of expression—so must we penetrate ours. We must enter into our world and its movements, not as a counterforce, but rather to shape and guide it according to the light of faith and sound reason.

Vincent Lebbe would pay a dear price for translating those brave words into brave deeds.

Vincent loved the seminary life. He studied, prayed and made friends—and he still clung to his dream of martyrdom in China. His family traveled down from Belgium occasionally. After each visit he suffered sharp bouts of loneliness. He had grown quite close, however, to Antoine Cotta, an Egyptian seminarian. With disarming directness he said to Cotta one day, "Help me to become a saint!" Cotta knew Lebbe meant every word of it—Vincent was too honest not to say what he meant. Cotta, a bit older, exercised a calming influence on the sometimes overenthusiastic Vincent. The Egyptian possessed a deep love and knowledge of St. Paul, the church's first great missionary. Sharing his knowledge with Vincent, he laid a scriptural underpinning to Vincent's missionary spirituality. The fire and zeal of St. Paul now combined with the calm, deliberate dedication of St. Vincent de Paul to shape Vincent's approach to his life as a missionary priest.

Cotta, ordained in June 1898, joined the Vincentian mission in Madagascar, an island off Africa's southeastern coast. The Egyptian would re-enter Lebbe's life and play a crucial role in later events.

About the same time as Cotta's ordination, Lebbe began to suffer a strange illness that caused general debilitation and dysentery. His superiors sent him to the Vincentian college at Dax, near the French coast, to continue his philosophy studies. There his condition worsened—he began to suffer pains in his chest and frequent nosebleeds. "I wonder," he worried, "if I have tuberculosis."

Frederick, right, entered the Vincentians in France, while his brother
Adrien entered the Benedictines in Belgium. Adrien became an abbot and
was highly respected for his knowledge of the liturgy.

His fears were not so much that the disease might take his life. He had
already expressed a desire for martyrdom. Rather, his worry rose out of the
very real possibility that his superiors would not permit him to be ordained
and go to China.

For the next year Lebbe's health continued to deteriorate. In
September 1900, seminary authorities advised him that his physical condition
disqualified him as a candidate for the missions. They further advised him he
could go to Rome and begin his studies in theology. "You can study," his
superiors added kindly, "at your own pace." It seemed now as if Vincent's
dreams of imitating his beloved Jean Gabriel Perboyre would never be realized.

At the same time Vincent's hopes for future martyrdom were being
dashed, many Europeans were dying in China. The Western nations had

secured, by manipulation and extortion, vast property holdings, called concessions, in various Chinese seaports and cities. In 1900 Chinese patriots, outraged by the relentless greed and oppression of these nations, rose in revolt against the Europeans and Americans. The frenzied Chinese massacred white men, women and children, set fire to Western business buildings, dock areas, and manufacturing plants. Because the Chinese revolutionaries, called Boxers, viewed the Christian missionaries as symbols of European and American hypocrisy, they turned on them in bitter revenge. They drove Protestant ministers and their families, Catholic priests, brothers and nuns from churches, schools, orphanages and hospitals. They murdered some; others were fortunate enough to escape to defense centers the Western powers quickly established in major Chinese cities. Western nations retaliated quickly by sending an army of 14,000 troops to quell the rebellion. The disciplined forces pounced upon the hapless rebels. The army cut an avenging swath of blood and fire through China and, in August 1900, entered Peking. Generals divided Peking into sectors and turned over a portion of the city to the troops of each participating nation. "The Chinese are now to be taught a final lesson," the officers advised their men. The troops rampaged through Peking, one of the world's most beautiful cities, leaving a trail of pillage, rape and wanton murder. When all the horror ended, peace was restored and European flags flapped once more in the breezes over China. Thirty thousand Christians had died—and a million non-Christians.

Shortly after the Boxer Rebellion ended Bishop Alphonse Favier, the French prelate of Peking, journeyed to Rome to report on the tragic events. He stayed at the Vincentian college where Vincent was studying. One evening after the bishop gave an unusually vivid description of the church's suffering during the revolt, Vincent approached him. With his customary enthusiasm and energy Vincent pleaded with the bishop to take him back to China with him. "Even if I can't be a priest, Your Excellency, I will learn the language and teach catechism."

"Eh, well," said the old man, "you wish to work—come along. Just get permission from your Vincentian superior in Paris."

The bishop himself advised Vincentian authorities in Paris that he would willingly accept young Lebbe even if his health was poor. "In China," the prelate said, "we need every hand we can get!" On February 10, 1901,

Bishop Favier brought Vincent to Peking.

exactly five months after his superiors advised him to forget a missionary career, Vincent Lebbe sailed out of Marseilles on the *S.S. Ernest Simons,* China-bound.

While on the month-long voyage a veteran missionary, Father Ponzi, introduced Vincent to the study of the Chinese language and customs. Vincent learned to write his name in Chinese letters. Eventually he translated his signature as "the thunder that sings in the distance." The name would someday be blessed and cursed throughout China.

Vincent arrived at the Vincentian mission headquarters in Peking in late March 1901. Despite chronic eye trouble which had begun during his illness at Dax, Vincent received permission to continue his studies for the priesthood. Perhaps someday he might be ordained.

At the Vincentian mission headquarters in Peking, Vincent encountered the deep division between Western missionaries and Chinese clergy that characterized the church in China. In the dining room Chinese clergy sat at one set of tables, Europeans at another. Both elements desired this. The Chinese preferred their own food and conversation in their native tongue to Western food and language. Few missionaries spoke Chinese very well; they preferred French in dinner conversation. Some missionaries never learned to read Chinese.

It was the heady days of the "White Man's Burden." Europeans and Americans judged themselves a superior breed whose destiny it was to lift inferior races (black, brown, red and yellow) out of their ignorance. Missionaries, products of Western civilization, absorbed this same attitude. They viewed the Chinese as mere children in the faith.

Missionaries in the 19th and 20th centuries had indeed given some consideration to elevating Chinese priests to the hierarchy. But the hierarchy of Lebbe's early career, composed exclusively of Westerners, judged such a step premature.

"When I was a young missionary," old Bishop Favier commented one day to Vincent, "I used to think we should have Chinese bishops. But as the years went on," he commented sadly, "I became convinced they are not yet ready."

Another factor that deepened the gulf between the Orientals and Westerners was the strong connection between the French government and the Catholic church. In France the anticlerical government scorned the church; in China the French government judged itself the protector of all Catholic missions and their personnel. The British served in the same capacity for the Protestant missionary effort. The French government urged each Catholic missionary to carry a French passport. This document would entitle him to call upon the French consul for protection. It also entitled the missionary to special privileges in Chinese law.

The French were all too ready to "protect" the missionaries and often used armed force to do so. French authorities used each incident of intervention on behalf of the missionaries to squeeze new concessions in law or property from the hapless Chinese. No wonder the Chinese spoke of two devils: Number One Devils were the foreigners and their missionaries; Number Two Devils were Chinese who had become Christians.

Vincent's finely honed sense of justice was outraged by the dependence of the church on the French government and even more dismayed by the readiness of French officials to exploit the situation. He had written, back in the seminary days in Paris: "We are to penetrate the modern world—not as a counterforce but rather to shape and guide it according to the light of faith and sound reason." From what he could determine, the missionary effort in China was failing because the missionaries were not entering into the Chinese world. They preferred to shape it according to the European models which the Chinese detested.

From the very beginning of his days in Peking, Vincent determined to join the Chinese world. "I know if I remain a European," he wrote, "I will end up a corpse."

Thus he recreated with Chinese student priests, took long walks with them, insisted they converse in Chinese with him, and cajoled them into teaching him to read and write the language. The young Chinese clerics were delighted.

Since eye trouble continued to plague him, Vincent's superiors sent him for a rest to An-kia-chwang, a village south of Peking. Because the town was all Christian, Boxers had struck viciously there during the rebellion. The Christians, however, well-armed and well-organized, drove off their attackers. But even now, guerrillas living in the hills sporadically raided An-kia-chwang. "It seems strange," Vincent wrote home, "to be in a theatre of war that is still smoking." Despite this, the village, with its Chinese architecture and, above all, its people, charmed Vincent. The only thing that disturbed him was the architectural style of the church right in the middle of town. "Built," he complained, "like a European church." Like all the other churches staffed by French missionaries, the church at Chwang flew the French flag on Sundays and holidays.

In the fall Vincent returned to Peking to resume his studies. His eye condition worsened. He made a novena to Blessed Jean Gabriel Peboyre, seeking a cure. His eyes cleared and remained sound until his death. Bishop Favier, who genuinely liked Lebbe despite his espousal of the Chinese cause, gave proper permissions, and Vincent was ordained a priest, October 28, 1901.

*   *   *   *   *

The Chinese Catholic Church that young Father Lebbe was ordained to serve had a long history. When Franciscan missionaries arrived in China in the 13th century, they were surprised to find Christian communities dating back several centuries. A form of Christianity called Nestorianism had been introduced into China, probably in the seventh century.

The Chinese of the 13th century received the friars kindly and several thousand accepted baptism. The Franciscans established a hierarchy, built churches and schools and even enjoyed honored positions in the court of the great Khan. The Khans were Mongolian overlords. Under Ghengis Khan and his son Ogedei, the Mongols conquered China, Persia, swept across Russia, occupied Poland and Hungary. The very word *Tartar*—a synonym for Mongol—struck such terror in the European heart that Pope Innocent IV ordered a new petition in the Litany of the Saints: "From the fury of the Tartars, deliver us, O Lord!" Just as the Tartars were about to deluge all of western Europe in fire and blood, Ogedei died. With his death in 1241 the Tartar hordes returned to Mongolia to elect a new leader.

In the middle of the 14th century the Chinese people rebelled against their Mongolian overlords, threw out the Khans, and installed their own rulers, called the Mings. The Ming dynasty, determined to eradicate all traces of foreign influence, began a systematic persecution of the church. So thoroughly did they ravage the Christians that when European missionaries returned in the 16th century all significant traces of Christianity had disappeared.

When Jesuit Father Matteo Ricci led a movement in the 16th century to adapt Christianity to Chinese customs, he came under severe attack from Rome. Conservative elements among Franciscans and other orders who worked with the poorer Chinese felt such a possibility would dilute Christianity beyond recognition. Ricci and the Jesuits had been enjoying phenomenal success in their missionary efforts among Chinese scholars and the wealthier classes. At the end of the 16th century the church numbered some 300,000 members in China. When Rome condemned the adaptation policy in 1715, Chinese Catholics and non-Catholics, sensitive to the beauty of their own culture and civilization, were profoundly insulted. Christians were killed. Prices were put on the heads of certain missionaries as agents of foreign governments. The sorest trials, however, were yet to come.

In the early 16th century Portuguese traders established, at gun point, a colony at Ningpo. The Chinese, who did not possess firearms, were unable, at first, to repel the invaders who wrested their lands from them. Soon after the conquest, Catholic missionaries arrived. In Chinese eyes these priests, by their presence, approved the seizure of Chinese lands.

Predictably the Chinese waited patiently and in 1545 turned on their conquerors massacring 12,000 Christians, most of whom were Chinese. The damage, however, had been done. The cause of Christianity and the foreign gun had been irrevocably linked in the Chinese mind.

Later events only reinforced the unfortunate association. In ensuing years, foreign power after foreign power pounced upon China to wrench privileges of ports and property from her. The missionaries who accompanied these incursions often sought the protection and assistance of the occupying nations.

Alongside the missionaries' confused leadership and the bad example of many Western Christians, there were always zealous priests, nuns and brothers who had no other desire than to love and serve the Chinese. It was these hidden and forgotten heroes who kept the flickering flame of faith alive in China.

Bishop Jarlin, the assistant who had ordained Vincent, took the new priest on a confirmation tour through the Peking Vicariate, which was as big as Belgium and Holland combined. Twelve million Chinese inhabited this district; 35,000 of them were Catholics.

For three weeks Vincent heard confessions, baptized and instructed. The tour was for him a precious learning experience. The effects of the Boxer Revolution were everywhere. He met Chinese who bore in their bodies the scars of persecution; others whose dear ones had died for the faith. Their simple, unpretentious love of their faith touched him so deeply that he wrote home to his brother: "You can't imagine what my life is like . . . what tremendous joy it gives me. . . . I have come to understand how the first Apostles felt and how St. Paul could write those wonderful letters. . . ."

*   *   *   *   *

Shortly after the year 1902 began, Bishop Jarlin appointed Vincent assistant pastor of Ta-k'ow-t'un, a rural mission 60 miles east of Peking. Now the new priest had full opportunity to carry out the brave words he wrote to a friend in Rome: "We only get to know people by becoming one with them; we only win them by giving ourselves. God is my witness that I shall spare nothing to gain that end."

He spared no effort to become Chinese. He studied the written language, paying particular attention to the classics and practiced conversation. He wore the garment of the poor Chinese, a cheap cloth robe. He adopted a pigtail and grew a beard.

"I'm out on the road all the time," he wrote, "on horseback, in carts, going from north to south, east to west, . . . one day feasting, one day fasting." His letters reflected his enthusiasm and energy. Even his poor health proved no obstacle. "How marvelous it is," he exclaimed in the same letter, "to live for God."

With his pigtail flying in the wind behind him as he bicycled between the rice paddies he became a picturesque figure in the country districts. He was full of energy and good humor. He spent happy hours sitting and smoking his long Chinese pipe with his farmer Christians.

The Chinese peasant is noted for hard and steady work. During planting, growing and harvesting seasons, the farmers worked seven days a week. Father Lebbe challenged his Christians to work only six. "God will do the rest," he advised them. After some hesitation one tiny congregation of Christians, in simple faith, accepted Lebbe's direction. When harvest time came, a disease attacked the crops. Although many crops died, the Christians' crops survived.

Bishop Jarlin ordained him.

In September 1906, Bishop Jarlin, now Vicar Apostolic after Favier's death, appointed Vincent director of the Catholic mission in Tientsin, North China's second largest city. Tientsin boasted a million people, including 15,000 Chinese Catholics. Jarlin, fully aware of Lebbe's enthusiasm for things Chinese, warned him that Tientsin was not the countryside. The city contained many European concessions and a consequent Chinese hatred of things European. "Keep out of political questions and do priestly work only," the bishop ordered him. "The situation is delicate."

Delicate indeed! For five days after he arrived in Tientsin, Vincent sat in the rectory mission waiting for a Chinese Christian to call. Not one came. Lebbe couldn't stand the quiet any longer and went out to find his scattered and concealed flock. He went from Christian home to Christian home, observing the elaborate Chinese etiquette, speaking the language well, dealing with each person as a fellow human being. He made every effort to meet Tientsin's Chinese officialdom, its intellectuals,

Father Lebbe saw the necessity for a Chinese church not independent of Europe. He immediately assumed local dress and grooming.

Father Lebbe soon after his arrival at Tientsin.

merchants and tradesmen. He extended great concern and charity to the poor and needy, whether Christian or not.

His zeal paid off. All elements of Tientsin's society soon made their way to the Vincentian mission to visit Father Lebbe. He opened a small mission center in the Chinese part of town, and more and more Chinese responded to his efforts. They came to him for help of every sort, spiritual and material, and he tried to respond. Moneys that he needed for his charities did not come from European sources alone, but in a great measure from the Chinese themselves. Garbed in his simple Chinese robe, he pedaled all over town, never ashamed to beg from anybody, particularly wealthy Chinese. He soon became a living legend in the city.

In July 1907 he organized a banquet for all his Chinese mission leaders. The banquet was extraordinary because European missionaries and

Chinese Christians had never shared the same table. Bishop Jarlin summoned Father Lebbe to Peking after the banquet and gave him a two-day dressing-down for permitting the fraternization. "You are showing off," the bishop charged, "and I want it stopped."

Why didn't the bishop just remove him? Jarlin secretly admired Father Lebbe. Bewildered, Lebbe returned to Tientsin and continued to do what he thought best. He encouraged various Chinese religious organizations, sponsored a vigorous convert movement called The Propagation of the Faith, and laid the groundwork for the first Catholic Action movement in China. He also established a number of lecture halls in the city. These provided a forum for Chinese priests and laymen to speak regarding contemporary Chinese problems.

In January 1912 he published the first issue of a Chinese Catholic

Lebbe established a number of lecture halls in Tientsin. Here he is pictured speaking in one of them.

weekly newspaper, *The Sunday Paper*. Everyone was delighted by it, that is, everyone except Bishop Jarlin who ordered the missionaries not to read it even though he had given permission for its publication. "I didn't know Father Lebbe would publish the paper," the bishop claimed. "I thought only lay people would do that!" In the end Jarlin gave a lukewarm approbation of it. Soon after, the Tientsin district was established as a separate diocese and the new bishop, Paul Dumond, gave the paper his enthusiastic support.

Under the new bishop, Lebbe's apostolic work expanded and flourished. Although Christians composed only one percent of Tientsin's population, they made their presence felt in every phase of the city's life. In the first Parliamentary elections held since the establishment of the new Chinese Republic in 1911, Christians gained 20 percent of the seats in Parliament for the Tientsin district.

In 1913 things were going well enough for Father Lebbe to return to Europe. He had been in China for 12 years and looked forward to his return home.

He spent about six months in Europe raising funds for his projects, particularly for the schools and institutions of higher learning he planned at Tientsin. Wherever he could get ears to listen, he would speak of the need to hand over the Chinese church to the Chinese clergy.

Two prominent European churchmen who listened to Lebbe's pleas were Monsignor Vanneufville, rector of the French Seminary in Rome, and Cardinal Mercier, Belgium's heroic prelate. These men put Father Lebbe in contact with Cardinals Bisletti and Gotti of the Roman Congregation of the Propagation of the Faith, the Vatican office charged with the proper conduct of the church's missionary effort.

In these highest circles the missioner continued to hammer out his theme: The Catholic church in China must become a Chinese church if it is to take a firm root in the nation. Now it is a Western church.

Early in 1914 he returned to Tientsin. Hundreds of Chinese crowded to the railroad station; when he descended from the train they burst into applause and shouted for joy.

He was back at work immediately, adding more and more activities to a list that would wear out a dozen men. In recognition of his highly successful work Bishop Dumond somewhat uneasily appointed him Vicar General of the Diocese of Tientsin.

The following fall Lebbe promoted the First National Congress of Catholic Action at Tientsin. Chinese Catholics and missionaries traveled from all over China to attend. Predictably, the Congress was well-organized and drew national attention. At the Congress Lebbe published the first Chinese Catholic daily, which he entitled *The Social Welfare*. Although published under Catholic auspices the paper was also aimed at non-Christian readers. *The Social Welfare* carried news of general interest, advertising of all kinds, and an editorial page. Lebbe wrote the daily editorial.

In Lebbe's mind the newspaper was to be a vehicle of truth. Whenever he complained that the church in China was too closely associated with the French government, fellow missionaries would respond, "But who will protect us?" For Lebbe truth was the greatest protection, and *The Social Welfare* would publish it. Within a few months of publication, Lebbe's daily was the most prestigious in North China.

* * * * *

Since his elevation in 1912, Bishop Dumond had had his own dreams. One of them was to lead to the unfortunate Lao-Si-Kai affair. Bishop Dumond wanted to provide the Tientsin diocese with a suitably large cathedral and commodious bishop's palace—constructed, of course, in European fashion. To achieve this he purchased a valuable piece of property in a newly

Vincent Lebbe holds up a copy of his Catholic daily newspaper, published for North China.

developing district of Tientsin. The area was so promising that the French consul had been attempting to wrest a section of it from Tientsin municipal authorities for several years. The Chinese refused to grant the concession, but the Tientsin municipal authorities willingly sold the property to the bishop for the cathedral and the palace.

After the bishop had title to the property, the consul dispatched French police to guard a new piece of roadway that lay in front of the cathedral. He felt justified in so doing because the mission procurator had entered into a secret deal with the consul. The priest had promised to cede the road and the land alongside it to the French if, in return, the consul would exempt the mission from any taxes when the district became French.

The presence of the French police, the attempt of the consul to levy taxes on the Chinese who had shops along the new roadway, and the secret deal itself, which eventually was revealed, threw Tientsin's Chinese population into an uproar. The Chinese who had shops and residences along the road refused to move, and Chinese police remained, despite the presence of the French. So far the land grab remained a standoff. Tientsin Chinese were furious. "Tricked again," they cried, "by those lying French and their missionaries!"

The Peking government protested. When Lebbe's newspaper, *The Social Welfare,* published an open letter asking the consul to drop his claims, that gentleman, outraged, demanded that Bishop Dumond silence the paper. Bishop Dumond ordered *The Social Welfare* to observe strict neutrality in the matter. Lebbe obeyed. By so doing, of course, he left only the non-Christian press in Tientsin to defend the Chinese rights.

To intimidate the bishop and pound the missionaries into line, the French consul conscripted one of the French priests. Because it was during World War I, the consul was within his rights. He ordered the priest into uniform and assigned him to guard duty in the French concession.

Despite the galling provocation, Bishop Dumond ordered all the missionaries to remain strictly neutral in the affair—to side neither with the Chinese nor the French.

Lebbe was furious and brokenhearted at the same time. He wrote a long personal letter to the French minister in Peking, Monsieur Conty, begging him to intervene. "The honor of France is at stake," he wrote. "Are we, for the sake of a bit of land, to surrender a heritage of esteem and affection?''

Conty returned the letter to Bishop Dumond and, in an angry note to the prelate, blamed him for allowing such an insolent and near traitorous letter to be written by one of his priests.

Dumond called Lebbe to his office and gave him a tongue-lashing and ordered him to say no more to anyone about the Lao-Si-Kai affair.

After the interview Lebbe asked to be sent away from Tientsin. "I beg you," he wrote, "do not leave me in such a position that I have either to disobey you or act in a way I regard as contrary to what my duty demands."

A few days later his Vincentian superiors notified Father Lebbe that he was transferred to the neighboring diocese of Chengting and ordered him to remain there with his old friend, Bishop de Vienne. The year was 1916. He was to spend his time in Chengting working with the poor. His superiors advised the priest to consult with Bishop de Vienne concerning his future.

Bishop de Vienne trusted and admired Lebbe but admittedly did not understand him. Nevertheless, he supported him bravely during his darkest hour. Vincent was disheartened, depressed and discouraged. For the first few weeks in Chengting, he kept to his room, but Bishop de Vienne gently nudged him back into apostolic activity. Within months Lebbe was in full swing, adapting his Tientsin methods to Chengting. But then de Vienne received a scathing letter from the Vincentian superior, Father Desrumaux. "We did not send Father Lebbe there for full apostolic work," Desrumaux wrote. "You make a laughing stock of Bishop Dumond by making Lebbe so important in Chengting."

In the meanwhile, back at Tientsin the Christians and non-Christians were dismayed by Lebbe's abrupt departure. They sought explanation from Bishop Dumond and Vincentian authorities. A delegation even journeyed into Vincentian headquarters at Peking on his behalf. But they received little consolation from either source.

Some priests headed by Father Cotta, who had left Madagascar and joined the Chinese missions a few years after Lebbe arrived in China, wrote to Vincentian authorities in Rome. After Lebbe was with Bishop de Vienne for some time, the Vincentian Council of the Northern Province restudied the Tientsin affair and exonerated Lebbe. The Paris headquarters of the Vincentians requested that Lebbe be returned to the Tientsin diocese.

Bishop Dumond acquiesced and wrote Lebbe at Chengting, inviting him to return and appointing him an assistant at Hokia, the smallest and most remote parish in the Tientsin diocese.

"When you pass through Tientsin on your way to Hokia you are not to leave the railway station," the bishop ordered. When news of the new appointment broke in Tientsin and other parts of Christian and non-Christian circles in China, letters flew to Rome and to Vincentian headquarters in Peking and Paris. Father Cotta and Father Yang, a Chinese priest, organized a formal complaint against Bishop Dumond and the Vincentian superiors. It was signed by 19 of Tientsin's 26 priests and sent to Rome. Accompanying the letter was a report giving the complete background on the case. The report indicated that Lebbe was being persecuted because he resisted "Europeanizing" the Chinese Catholic Church.

While all this was happening, the Lao-Si-Kai affair took a nasty turn when French troops occupied the area, drove out the Chinese police, and claimed the territory for France. From faraway Hokia, Lebbe bombarded:

> If I were a civilian, I would give everything I possess to buy gunpowder and cannon balls and die in Lao-Si-Kai. . . . But since we are priests let us swear once again to die in Rome rather than keep silent in the face of evil.

Lebbe's old friend, Monsignor Vanneufville, rector of the French seminary in Rome, advised Lebbe by letter that his case was receiving full consideration by proper authorities in Rome. In March the Vincentians sent a special visitator, Father Guilloux, to Tientsin to investigate the complaints in the Roman letter against Bishop Dumond. After some interviews Guilloux called all the priests together (including Lebbe) and excoriated them. The visitator charged that by siding with the Chinese they were destroying a 300-year-long honorable tradition of mission service and promoting a possible schism in the Chinese Catholic Church.

As Lebbe listened to the visitator, he knew beyond doubt a reconciliation was impossible. As long as Europeans felt sole responsibility for the missions, there would never be a Chinese Catholic Church.

Bewildered and depressed, Lebbe returned to Hokia. He would continue to conscientiously tend his little corner of the vineyard and wait for the Lord to show him what to do. Passion Sunday was coming and with it Holy

The young seminarian would mature into an enthusiastic, influential missionary. He would go by the name Vincent.

Week. There were Catholic Action meetings to plan, instruction centers to organize, Masses to say.

On the Saturday evening before Passion Sunday Lebbe received the fateful note removing him from Hokia in the Tientsin diocese and sending him to a mission a thousand miles away. He spent the night in agony; should he capitulate or not? On Passion Sunday he had made up his mind. He would remain obedient unto death. He wrote his superiors and accepted the transfer without a murmur or sign of rebellion. Yet the anguish was there. He wrote to a friend, "I am writing in an abyss of agony."

Many other priests who organized the letter of complaint to Rome were also transferred that same weekend to posts far from Tientsin diocese. Lebbe's movement for a Chinese Catholic Church was stopped dead.

*   *   *   *   *

Once more Father Lebbe was on the move. This time he was to go to Ning-po in South China. His new superior, Bishop Reynaud, was a man full of compassion and love for the Chinese. He welcomed Father Lebbe and respected him for his accomplishments and also for his love of religious obedience.

With Reynaud's backing, Lebbe was soon repeating his Tientsin successes. Reynaud appointed him director of the Shao-king district—a major post.

Rome continued to keep abreast of events in China and express its deep concern about the extent of European influence in the missionary effort. On November 30, 1919, Pope Benedict XV issued an important statement regarding the issue. In brief, the pope called upon missionaries to labor for a native clergy, a native hierarchy, a native church. He condemned the attitude of missionaries who "think rather of their earthly country than of the heavenly." They make the church appear to the people among whom they labor, the pope continued, "as a religion that belongs to some foreign nation rather than the Kingdom of Heaven."

The letter landed like a bomb among the French bishops in China. They reacted predictably. "The Holy Father has been misinformed," they complained. "To follow out his program in China would right now provoke a schism."

Lebbe, now full of new hope and new strength, experienced new frustration. He knew the bishops would drag their feet in complying with the pope's directions, and he was right. "In fifty years," one learned bishop announced, "these directions of the pope might possibly be fulfilled."

Rome continued its interest in the Chinese question by appointing a series of visitators who journeyed through the missions and sent a steady stream of reports back to the Vatican. Two of the visitators, both members of the French Foreign Mission Society, Bishop de Fouquet and Archbishop de Guebriant, bluntly advised Lebbe to leave China if he wished Rome to consecrate Chinese bishops. "You have become a center of controversy," the visitators told him. "There are few missionaries who support you. If you go, tempers will calm and we can approach the question in a more reasonable manner."

When Vincentian authorities offered in 1920 to send Lebbe to Europe to organize the large number of Chinese studying in the continent's universities, he accepted. Although he understood his superiors were only too glad to have him leave China, he was not adverse to going. The job needed doing, and the trip would enable him to renew contacts in Rome.

For the next seven years he crisscrossed Europe in search of young Chinese. He helped them with room, board, and tuition; organized them into groups; and made contact with many young people who eventually became their nation's leaders. Always and everywhere he was their beloved pastor, concerned only with their best interests.

During these years he pressed his campaign for a native hierarchy wherever he could get an audience. Indeed, in 1920, Cardinal Mercier, deeply interested in the Chinese question, had summoned Lebbe to Rome. This was the first link in an unbelievable chain of events. Mercier sent Lebbe to Cardinal Willem Van Rossum, head of the Congregation of the Propagation of the Faith. The interview concluded with Van Rossum requesting names of some possible Chinese priests as candidates for bishops. Cardinal Van Rossum thanked Lebbe for his years of suffering and added, "It was your obedience that saved everything . . . that was what God gave his blessing to."

A few days after Christmas 1920, Pope Benedict summoned Lebbe for a private audience. The pope assured the missionary that he would follow up with the appointment of the Chinese bishops. Lebbe could hardly believe all this was happening. "There are hours in life," he later exclaimed, "that can compensate for years of suffering." Benedict was to die in 1922 and Pius XI become pope before the appointments came through. It took four years, fraught with dashed hopes, before Pope Pius XI consecrated six Chinese bishops in St. Peter's.

Lebbe, because he had no special place for the ceremony, arrived early at St. Peter's to get a good seat. He wept quietly throughout the Mass. He was 25 years a priest on the very day of the consecration. No missionary could ever be given a more magnificent anniversary gift.

At a banquet that evening three Chinese bishops sat at Lebbe's right, three at his left. He was in his proper place.

*   *   *   *   *

The crowning moment of Vincent Lebbe's life came when he watched Pope
Pius XI consecrate these six men as China's first native bishops.

Lebbe returned to China in 1927 and was assigned Diocesan Director
of Catholic Action in the diocese of Bishop Sun, one of the newly consecrated Chinese. He worked with great zest and joy in rural Hopeh, Sun's
diocese. European bishops and missionaries, however, ostracized him. He
bore this with grace, and he continued pioneering.

In 1928 he founded two religious orders: one for men called the Little
Brothers of St. John the Baptist; the other for women, the Little Sisters of
St. Therese of the Child Jesus. He drew up a way of life for each that was
strict and austere. He led the way by the example of his own life of prayer
and penance. On Christmas 1933 he decided to leave the Vincentians and
became the head of the Little Brothers.

Although he was 56 years old, he continued moving about Hopeh on
his bicycle. He was known to pedal 100 kilometers a day. Now, however, he

began to fall off the bike from time to time, badly injuring knees and arms. He underwent two operations as a result of these falls, but he continued to bicycle. "It is," he stated, "the poor man's manner of travel."

*   *   *   *   *

In 1931 the Japanese had invaded Manchuria and set off a series of wars which involved China for the next 25 years. When all the fighting was done, China emerged as a Communist nation.

Lebbe, of course, didn't know that. All he knew when war broke out was that his people were suffering. During the endless fighting that swept back and forth over the tortured land, Lebbe played a major part in treating the wounded and war refugees. He recruited hundreds of Chinese Christians and non-Christians to serve as stretcher-bearers. Indeed, before the war concluded his band of stretcher-bearers numbered 20,000. Lebbe, no pacifist, urged the Chinese to fight bravely for their country. At Chiang Kai-shek's request he traveled through the countryside rallying the people to the defense of their land against the Japanese invaders. Although he refused to carry a weapon of any kind and dismissed one of his Little Brothers for packing a revolver, he trained guerrilla bands to strike against the Japanese. They proved tough and effective.

Stretcher-bearing was exhausting work. In one mountain battle the bearers had to carry the wounded as far as 10 miles before they could get help. They rescued 800 men; they also buried 700. Despite all the backbreaking work, Lebbe insisted he and the Little Brothers recite the prayers of the Divine Office daily. The hardship and danger eventually took their toll of poor Father Lebbe. The bicycle falls now made their effects felt in arthritic pain; he was often feverish with exhaustion.

In the spring of 1940 Father Lebbe and six of his Little Brothers were arrested by elements of the Eighth Communist Chinese Army. Up until this point Lebbe had enjoyed good relations with the Chinese Communists. But as relations between the Reds and Chiang Kai-shek deteriorated, the Communists, who had begged Lebbe to join them, began to fear him and his Little Brothers as agents of Chiang Kai-shek.

Although the Reds did not treat their prisoners cruelly, Lebbe's health deteriorated rapidly during the several weeks he was a Communist hostage. Finally, when Chiang Kai-shek threatened to free Lebbe by force, the Communists released him and his group of Little Brothers.

After three weeks' walk through Japanese lines, Lebbe arrived safely at Loyang. He was worn out. His internal organs, his kidneys, liver and stomach, were all swollen. He was full of jaundice. "Look," he joked, "I'm finally yellow. I'm no longer a white man."

The physical anguish was compounded when he discovered the Communists had murdered 12 of his Little Brothers. Lebbe could not believe that the Chinese, even the Communists, could be so cruel as to harm these gentle, courageous men.

Chiang Kai-shek sent a plane to bring Lebbe to Chungking. There, in the home of a Chinese friend and surrounded by Chinese, Vincent Lebbe died on June 24, 1940, the feast of St. John the Baptist. He was 62. No one made particular note at the time, but June 24 was also the feast of Blessed Jean Gabriel Perboyre. It was Perboyre who had moved the 11-year-old Freddy years before to announce, "I want to go to China and die a martyr's death."

Bishop Paul Yu Pin blessed Vincent's body before his burial in Chungking. Yu Pin eventually became a cardinal.

Franz Jaegerstaetter

Franz Jaegerstaetter had finished work on his farm in St. Radegund, a tiny village in the Salzach region of Upper Austria. Standing for a moment in the evening silence, he watched the sun turning the sky into a glorious pink and pastel-blue canopy. His heart lightened by the beauty above, he put away his tools and set out for the village tavern. He would enjoy a drink before returning home to his wife, Francesca, and infant daughter, Rosalie.

As he made his way to the tavern he felt the gentleness of the breeze dancing lightly through the village. The surrounding fields, already plowed and planted, were full of promise. The trees in a copse near the village, their boughs and leaves cleansed by winter snows and April's cold rains, turned gold in the evening sun. Franz, hearing a cuckoo cry in the distance, remembered with a smile the old proverb, Whoever hears the cuckoo will always have money in his pocket.

At the tavern he was greeted by an old friend and fellow farmer whom he joined for a drink and conversation about farm topics and local news. Despite a stubborn streak inherited from his mother, Franz's winning and lighthearted manner had won him the genuine affection of the villagers. This feeling prompted his friend to steer their conversation into a serious channel.

"Franz, I'm worried about you. There's word all over the village that you've been denouncing Hitler again at an inn near Linz."

Franz laughed and responded, "You know what I think of the whole Nazi gang."

"Yes, not only do I know what you think of the whole Nazi gang, but everybody in Upper Austria knows what you think about the whole Nazi gang. Franz, these Nazis have spies everywhere. They kill people for saying less than what you say."

Franz laughed again, but then turned serious. "The Nazis are bad men," he said. "Believe me, they will destroy not only Germany, but our beloved Austria as well."

"Franz, we had no choice but to allow them to take over Austria," his friend said, referring to German occupation of the country in March 1938. The takeover, or *Anschluss,* had just been ratified by Austrian voters in a plebiscite.

"Look, Franz," the man continued, "Hitler took the German people, beaten and demoralized, destroyed by the Treaty of Versailles, and made them a proud nation. The whole world now respects Germany. Hitler gave the people jobs, put food on their tables, beat inflation."

"We will pay a terrible price for this," Franz replied.

"You have your opinion," the companion countered, "but please keep it to yourself. You will get into trouble. Play the game."

"I cannot play the game," Franz responded sadly. "The game is a lie."

Both men had finished their drinks by this time. They rose to leave.

"Heil Hitler, Franz!" the friend gently saluted.

"Phooey Hitler!" answered Franz, a big smile lighting his face.

*   *   *   *   *

Born May 20, 1907, Franz was the illegitimate son of Franz Bachmeier and Rosalie Huber. Bachmeier supported Rosalie and Franz until he died in combat during World War I. Three years later Rosalie married

Herr Jaegerstaetter, owner of a St. Radegund farm known as the Leherbauer property.

As young Franz grew into manhood, he worked hard during the day on the farm and played hard during the night with his fellow villagers. He ran with a gang of toughs who, like their counterparts in other places, drank a lot of beer and fought against rival gangs from other villages. Their battles were often bloody. The gangs armed themselves with heavy chains and leather thongs filled with sand and edged with knife blades. Franz—quick-thinking, enthusiastic and courageous—emerged as a natural leader of the young ruffians of St. Radegund.

He and other members of the gang were arrested, fined and detained for a few days in 1934 for fighting with border patrolmen over the attentions and affections of young girls of the village.

Franz astride his motorcycle in front of his family home at St. Radegund. From the left—his half sister, mother and stepfather.

In the mid-1930s, Franz (*second from right, back row*) posed with his
fellow employees from the Steiermark iron mines.

Twenty-seven-year-old Franz left St. Radegund abruptly in 1934 amid
allegations that he had fathered an illegitimate child. Whether he did or not
is not certain. He did, however, support the mother and child from the earn-
ings of his job in the Steiermark iron mines. According to some who knew
him, this did not prove he was the child's father. Despite a wild streak he was
a generous young man, and it would not have been unlike him to help someone in trouble even if it cast a shadow on his reputation.

During his three years in the mines Franz experienced a religious conversion. He began to attend Mass and receive communion regularly. He cut
down on his drinking and carousing, developed a desire for prayer and
spiritual reading, and even thought seriously about entering the religious life.
A priest discouraged him, however, reminding him that he was the only sup-

port of his father and mother. "You must farm the Leherbauer property and take care of your parents," he was told.

In a letter of spiritual counsel written to his godson about this time, Franz revealed dissatisfaction with his past life and the movement toward God now taking place in his heart.

> You, too, will be experiencing the storms of youth. To some the storms come later than to others; to some they burst forth in full fury, while to others the onset is weak. Should it be that temptation is so strong that you feel you must give in to sin, give then some thought to eternal happiness. It often happens that a man risks his temporal and eternal happiness for a few seconds of pleasure. . . . This much I can tell you from my own experience.
>
> As long as we fear men more than God, we will never make the grade. Even the most courageous and best Christians can and do fall, but they do not lie for long in the filth of sin. Instead, they pull themselves together and draw new strength from the sacraments of penance and holy communion, and strive on to their eternal goal. Should anxious days come upon us when we feel we are being crushed under the weight of our troubles, let us remember that God burdens none of us with a heavier cross than we can bear.

Surprising advice coming from one who had justly earned a reputation as one of St. Radegund's "lively" citizens!

Sometime in 1936 Franz returned to St. Radegund. He continued reorganizing his life and deepening his relationship with God. Gone were the days and nights of drinking and carousing, dancing and fighting. His fellow villagers were amazed to learn that he had settled down.

He married a devout and lovely young woman. The couple honeymooned in Rome. At a general papal audience he and Francesca received the blessing of Pope Pius XI. Returning home Franz became a model husband.

His workday began at 5:30 a.m. He spent the early part of the morning in prayer and meditation and attended Mass and received communion daily. Anxious to make reparation for his former wild life, he did continual penance. He gave up beer, although he continued to drink strong cider on occasion; he fasted until noon each day; he gave generously to the poor.

Although the people of St. Radegund were sincere Catholics, they

thought Franz was a fanatic because of his daily attendance at Mass and reception of holy communion.

Franz found true peace and joy in his new manner of life. While working in the fields he occasionally broke into song. While resting from his work he often sat under a tree and read the Bible. He was vividly aware of the presence of God in the natural wonders which his beloved Austria possessed in such abundance.

*   *   *   *   *

Franz despised the Nazi movement and took advantage of every opportunity to speak out against it. Father Karobath, the local pastor and Franz's spiritual director, admired the farmer's outspoken opposition to the Nazi regime. When Franz resigned from the National Austrian Farmers Association in public protest against the organization's weakening opposition to Nazism, the pastor and many villagers praised him but warned that he was flirting with danger.

In April 1938 Austrians were to vote to approve or disapprove the German occupation of their country. Franz told Father Karobath, "I am going to vote No."

Franz and Francesca Jaegerstaetter on their wedding day, April 9, 1936.

"Franz, you know how much I hate Nazis. To vote No, however, is silly," the pastor responded. "First of all you will identify yourself as an opponent of the regime and—believe me—they will get you. If the vote is one hundred percent Austrian for the German takeover, people in the outside world will know the vote is a farce. Franz, as your pastor, I advise you to vote Yes."

"Pastor Karobath," Franz responded, "I respect and love you as a priest of God, but my conscience will not let me vote Yes."

"Franz, do what your conscience tells you to do. But, God help you. I hope you are prepared for the consequences of this action. You must keep in mind," the priest continued, "that you are not alone. You have a wife; you have a daughter and another child on the way; you have your parents depending on you."

"I know this, good Father. It pains me. But I cannot lie. The Hitler regime is evil. It will drive our people to do evil things. Besides, Father, I believe that God asks me to live by my conscience. If I do what I think he wants me to do, then I know he will take care of my wife, my children and all my responsibilities."

The Austrian people voted nearly unanimously on April 10 to accept Nazi rule of their homeland.

"I believe that what took place in the spring of 1938 was not much different," Franz wrote later, "from what happened that Holy Thursday nineteen hundred years ago when the crowd was given a free choice between the innocent Savior and the criminal Barabbas."

Franz continued his open opposition to the Nazi regime. He refused to contribute to the endless collections politicians were making for various causes. Only once did he contribute, and that was for a benefit for the police department. He explained, "I gave those poor fellows plenty of trouble; I owe them something."

He refused any benefits the new government provided the Austrian people. He was the only farmer who did not accept government-supplied produce in the wake of a disastrous hailstorm which destroyed most of the crops in the St. Radegund area.

Late in 1939 Franz was drafted into the Austrian army and assigned to the motorized corps. He spent seven months in training but was then deferred, probably because he was a farmer.

Franz (*third from left*) spent seven months training in a motorized division, but was then deferred.

His brief military experience convinced him that he could never serve in the army of the Third Reich. "If they call me up, I will not serve," he told his wife on his return to St. Radegund.

While Franz was away on military duty Father Karobath excoriated the Nazis during a Sunday homily. The regime had him removed immediately from St. Radegund. He was sent into early retirement and kept under surveillance by the Nazis. Father Furthauer was appointed to replace him.

When Franz returned home the new pastor noticed his sincerely devout life and asked him to assume the duties of parish sacristan. He gratefully accepted. Sacristan was a position of no small importance in St. Radegund whose population was almost totally Roman Catholic. Franz took his duties very seriously, keeping the church, which was built in 1642, in perfect order. As sacristan he ushered at Sunday Masses. He did so most conscientiously, angering some parishioners because he closed the doors the moment Mass started. When he reopened the doors to admit the latecomers their tardiness became known to the whole congregation. He trained altar boys well. No youngster would dare be late for a Mass assignment. Under his zealous coaching the village acolytes recited the Latin responses perfectly and carried out the rubrics carefully.

Meanwhile, Francesca gave birth to their second child, Marie. Franz, by hiring extra help, was able to continue cultivating the Leherbauer property and fulfilling his responsibilities as sacristan.

Although his days were filled with activity, Franz continued to struggle within himself. He sought to discover what God required of him regarding his duty to serve in the army. Father Furthauer, admitting he was unable to resolve Franz's problem, suggested that he consult other priests. Franz did this. He even visited the bishop of the Diocese of Linz. Every priest, without exception, advised him to report for military service if called up. Their judgment was based on this reasoning: His refusal to serve would make little or no difference to the Nazi war machine. However his death—the law demanded capital punishment for those who refused to serve—would bring grave harm to his wife and children.

Both his mother and his wife pleaded with him to answer the call. "Franz," his mother pointed out, "you will not necessarily have to kill if you go to war."

"This uniform," conscript Jaegerstaetter remarked to friends, "forces me to participate in a lie."

Word of his anti-regime attitude reached the police chief, a kind and fatherly man. "Franz," he advised, "I'll try to get you a noncombatant post. Please don't put me in the position of having to arrest you."

Some people suggested that he hide in the woods of the Salzach region. One man did so in the following year, a deserter from the village who was cared for by the people to such an extent that a local dentist went to his hideout and extracted an aching tooth.

Franz was willing to accept execution for himself; he understandably had difficulty in accepting the consequences of his death for his wife and family. "When one argues from the standpoint of the family," he told himself, "one cannot be troubled. One is not permitted to lie even for the sake of one's family. If I had 10 children, the greatest demand upon me is still the one I must make of myself."

Again and again friends stressed his obligations toward his wife and children. "I cannot believe that just because one has a wife and children," he would respond, "he is free to offend God. Did not Christ himself say, 'He who loves father, mother or children more than me is not deserving of my love'?"

In February 1943 the government ordered Franz to report for military service at the barracks in Enns, Austria. It was the moment of decision. Franz advised his wife that he could not be part of the blood bath into which the Nazis had plunged Europe. He told her he would refuse to take the oath of loyalty to Hitler when he reported for service. She wept. Franz dearly loved her and their three little girls (another daughter had been born), but he simply could not play what he called "the crooked game." He reported on March 4 to Enns, not wanting to embarrass St. Radegund's police chief who would otherwise have had to arrest him.

Immediately after arriving at Enns, Franz refused to take the military oath. Without hesitation the army sent him to the military prison at Linz. German military justice was harsh and prompt. He knew they could execute him at any moment. He lived his life hour by hour, meditating, praying the Rosary and reading spiritual books.

Shortly before leaving St. Radegund, Franz had written to "retired" Father Karobath:

I beg you to remember me at Mass as long as you are permitted to offer Mass. From my heart, I ask you to pray for me too, and to forgive me any trouble I may have ever caused you. May God not abandon me in this last hour. . . . God and the Blessed Virgin will surely not abandon my family when I can no longer protect them myself. Things will be very hard for my dear ones.

In his first letter home from prison Franz expressed his deep concern for the family. "Please do not forget me in your prayers," he begged. "Everything will turn out for the best according to God's will." His customary humor reappeared when he sent loving greetings from his "new home" to the family. "May God give you everything you desire for yourself," he also wrote to his wife, "as long as it is not likely to be a hindrance to your eternal welfare."

In another letter, a few days later, he provided glimpses of life in the military prison as he described bitter and disillusioned soldiers who had been thrown into prison for minor offenses. "It is frightful what these prisoners can tell you about what they have already done and suffered during these five years of war," he wrote. Soldiers received long sentences but could obtain release by volunteering for combat, especially at the Russian front. Many preferred prison, some even accepted death rather than go back to the eastern battle lines.

His concern turned again to his family. "When people ask you if you agree with my decision not to fight," he told his wife, "just tell them how you honestly feel. If I did not have such a great horror of lies and double-dealing, I would not be sitting here."

Authorities had questioned him about the advice given him by Father Karobath. Franz had been able to tell his interrogators that the pastor had advised him to accept military duty. However, he wrote his wife, "I am certain Pastor Karobath will not be free much longer."

A letter written the following week revealed that Franz's morale had suddenly dropped and his resolution had weakened. "I am troubled by the fear that you have so much to suffer on my account," he told his wife. "I worry about bringing injustice down upon you"

Although he had previously refused to serve in any unit of the army, even the medical corps where he would not have to harm anyone, he told Francesca at this point, "I can tell you that I have declared myself ready to serve in the medical corps." Nothing came of this request, and Franz somehow renewed his resolve not to serve at all.

Franz's refusal aroused a variety of responses in St. Radegund. Father Karobath judged him a hero. The priest infuriated many villagers by suggesting that they should have done exactly the same. Some friends and neighbors thought Franz's religious enthusiasm had softened his brain. Although some people accepted Franz's opposition to Hitler, many interpreted his deeds as a shirking of his duty to the Fatherland. No doubt his wife had to bear the scorn of people who were bearing the full brunt of the war, a war that had spared no family in the village. A few harshly judged him to be a criminal. He wrote of this to his wife:

> You should not be sad because of my present situation. For we cannot know God's mind or which of the many paths he leads us to travel. As long as a man . . . has an untroubled conscience and knows that he is really not a criminal, he can live in peace, even in prison.

Franz missed his beloved St. Radegund and the old church he had served so faithfully. In the cold and bare military prison at Linz he remembered the beauty of the liturgical services in the tiny village church. During Lent he united his sufferings with the sufferings of Christ and Mary.

Francesca told him that their oldest daughter, not yet 6 years old, wished to make sacrifices for him. Deeply touched, he wrote: "The sacrifices of our Rosalie will not be in vain. How could I feel abandoned here when so many are praying for me at home?"

It seemed that Rosalie's prayers strengthened and consoled her father and stiffened his resolve. From this point on his letters were cheerful and encouraging. He asked for envelopes and religious pamphlets, and, ever the farmer, he gave advice concerning spring planting.

He kept all of the feast days with special devotion. He described one, the feast of the Annunciation, as "that lovely day in which Christ assumed human form out of love for us men." Then he added: "There is practically nothing to do here in prison, but that does not mean that I have to let my days pass by without putting them to some use. As long as I can pray, and there is plenty of time for that, my life is not in vain.''

Besides his prayers, Franz found time to express in writing his reflections concerning the Nazi movement and his responsibilities as a Catholic in the face of the war that had engulfed Europe. This brief set of reflections, plus his prison letters and a notebook he compiled as a catechism for his godson, enabled a later generation to pierce some of the profound mystery surrounding his life and death. His love of freedom rings through these documents.

> My thoughts are being set down here as they come from my mind and heart. And, if I must write them with my hands in chains, I find that much better than if my world were in chains. In a prison, no chains, not even a sentence of death, can rob a man of the faith and his own free will. God gives so much strength that it is possible to bear any suffering, a strength far stronger than all the might of the world. The power of God cannot be overcome.

He wrote with clarity and directness. With a sharp and devastating blade of simplicity he cut through the fine web of theological reasoning that permitted a Catholic to support the war. He saw the frightful

The Jaegerstaetter girls. Christmas Day, 1941.

tragedy as the inevitable result of the paganism that both Allied and Axis powers served. As a citizen of the kingdom of heaven he could in no way serve the powers of darkness.

> Just as a man who thinks only of this world does everything that is possible to make life easier and better, so must we Christians who believe in the eternal kingdom risk everything in order to receive a great reward there. Just as those who believe in the Nazi platform tell themselves their struggle is with the Bible, so must we too convince ourselves that our struggle is for the eternal kingdom. There is this difference: We need no rifles or pistols for battle, but instead spiritual weapons; and the foremost among these is prayer. "For prayer," as St. Clare says, "is the shield which the flaming arrow of the Evil One cannot pierce." St. Clare constantly implored new grace from God, since, without God's help and grace, it would be impossible for us to preserve the faith and be true to his Commandments.

He also wrote:

> The true Christian is to be recognized more in his works and deeds than in his speech. . . . The surest mark of all is found in deeds.

And:

> To do unto one's neighbor what one would desire for himself means more than merely avoiding harm to our neighbor. We must love our enemies, bless those who curse us, pray for those who persecute us—and God's love will conquer and will endure for all eternity. Happy are they who live and die in God's love.

Franz's writings also contain an account of a harrowing experience he suffered after his marriage.

He had trouble falling asleep one summer night. He lay in bed until midnight, a most uncommon experience for a hard-working farmer. Then he fell into some kind of half-sleep.

> All of a sudden I saw a beautiful, shiny railroad train that circled around the mountains of Austria. Desiring to board the train, children and adults rushed toward it and could not be held back. I would rather not say how many adults did not

join the ride. Then I heard a voice say to me, "This train is going to hell." Immediately it seemed as if someone took me by the hand and said, "Now we will go to purgatory." Oh! so frightful was the suffering I saw and felt, I could only guess that I was in hell itself if the voice had not told me we were going to purgatory. Probably no more than a few seconds passed while I saw all this. I woke up and heard a sigh and saw a light, and all was gone. I woke up my wife right away and told her what had happened. Until that night I never would have believed that the suffering in purgatory could be so great.

*   *   *   *   *

Franz's kindness and warm personality won him many friends among the unfortunate inmates. One cellmate, a Frenchman, remembered:

We found a good friend in Franz, one who in the darkest moment was always able to provide a word of comfort and managed to give us his last piece of bread from the meager morning and evening meals we took in the cell. . . . His faith in God and justice was beyond measure unless one saw him sunk in prayer the whole day through, his rosary his constant companion. In the same way, the Easter communion we received together in April 1943 brought him great happiness.

Franz's mother, Rosalie, his daughters, Marie, Aloisia and Rosalie, and his wife, Francesca.

Most of the prisoners could not understand his refusal to serve in the army; however, they attested to his charity, good humor and faithfulness to his religion. He extended as much kindness as he could to those with whom he was living in the shadow of death.

On one occasion he wrote to his wife:

> I have another request to make of you. I wonder if maybe you could enclose a few edelweiss in your next letter? One of my comrades here asked if I might be able to get some for him. He is a young Frenchman who was sentenced last week. He would like to send the edelweiss to his girl friend as a remembrance, since she is very fond of flowers.

According to custom, a young man would climb a high mountain peak to pick edelweiss, the national flower of Austria, for his sweetheart as a sign of his love and devotion. Franz raised the spirits of his fellow prisoner with this bit of Austrian folklore and the request he made of Francesca.

Franz continued to worry about the children—Rosalie, Marie and Aloisia—and the consequences of his actions upon them. "I think it is better for you to tell the children where their father is," he suggested to Francesca, "rather than to lie to them."

He wrote to the children:

> I think of you very often and pray for you too. It would make me so happy if I could see you again. I would gather you all together so that you would soon learn not to fight among yourselves any more. Also, you must not lie. And, in the meantime, you should always be satisfied with what you get. Then I believe the heavenly Father will grant that I may come home to you someday, even though it may not be right away. My dear little girls, may the Child Jesus and the dear Mother of Heaven protect you until we all see each other again.

When Francesca suggested that she visit him, Franz, dreading the parting that would follow, responded:

> I would advise against it now. I have had no hearing yet and there is no decision in my case. It would certainly be a great joy to see you again, but I would still advise you to put the visit off for now. Dearest wife, let us carry our cross further with patience until God takes it from us.

In April, while still awaiting action on his case, Franz wrote to Francesca:

> Today it is seven years since we spoke our vows of love and fidelity before God and the priest. . . . When I look back upon all the joy . . . that has been mine these seven years, it seems at times to border on the miraculous. If someone were to tell me there is no God or that God does not love us, and if I were to believe him, I would not be able to explain how all this has come to me. Dearest wife . . . if only we do not forget to give thanks and do not hold ourselves back in striving for heaven, God will permit our joy to continue on for all eternity.
>
> As I sit behind prison walls I still believe I can build further on your love and devotion in days to come. . . . Now your dear husband greets you from his heart. I have been renewed because, it is said, human beings are completely renewed every seven years. From this day forth you have a new husband!

During Holy Week Franz immersed himself in meditation on the suffering and death of Christ. A priest came into the prison on Holy Thursday and Holy Saturday and brought communion to him. The Eucharist filled him with new hope. He wrote to Francesca:

> What is more joyous than the fact that Christ has risen again and has gone before us as victor over death and hell? What can give us Christians greater comfort than the knowledge that we never again need fear death?

Sensitive to nature, even in prison, Franz derived deep consolation from hearing birds singing in the prison courtyard and seeing springtime grass through the barred windows.

Father Franz Baldinger, a chaplain at the prison, visited Franz. He recalled him later as a fine, upstanding and brave man. Father Baldinger also attempted to dissuade Franz from his stance against military service.

"You must keep your own and your family's welfare in mind," he counseled. "You have no responsibility as a private citizen for the acts and policy of this government. If you take the oath and perform the services required, you will not be endorsing the Nazis and their objectives; instead, you will merely be following orders like millions of other Catholics, including

The village church, St. Radegund.

priests and seminarians. You have neither the facts nor the competence to pass final judgment as to the justice or injustice of this war.''

Franz had heard all the arguments before. Military authorities at the prison presented the same argument. They added a special twist.

''We are not asking you to fight for this regime,'' they said. ''We are demanding that you fight for the Fatherland. You must love your land. Do you want to see the Russians invade Austria, rape your women and burn your farm?''

*   *   *   *   *

On one occasion he attempted to explain his position with a parable. He described a farmer who found a little worm while digging in his garden.

The farmer had the choice of letting the worm live or cutting it in two with a stroke of his spade, for no cause and without justice. "Hitler is the farmer," Franz explained. "He willfully disposes of the lives of those he oppresses. The Nazi system cannot last long and is opposed to my Catholic religion."

At another time Franz advised an inmate that the war was doomed in advance. "As a Christian," he said, "I prefer to do my fighting with the word of God and not with arms. I love my country intensely and I will not serve anyone who oppresses Austria."

He preferred to suffer the brutal consequences of his stand rather than do evil to others. Yet the possibility that his action was equivalent to suicide deeply troubled Franz. During his Holy Week meditation on the passion of Christ, he became preoccupied with the possibility that he was committing mortal sin by his stand. He felt like Christ in the Garden of Gethsemane, and he united himself with all those who were suffering. He wrote home:

> If the cross that God has laid upon me becomes heavy, it will never get as difficult and heavy as the one that Satan loads on his followers, many of whom have already broken under this burden and thrown their lives away by suicide. . . .

He begged his wife never to pass judgment on a suicide:

> . . . The act is evil, but the person who commits it must be left to the hands of God. . . .

The letter also reflected his hope, however:

> . . . Easter is coming and, if it should be God's will that we can never again in this world celebrate Easter together in our intimate family circle, we can still look ahead in the happy confidence that, when the eternal Easter morning dawns, no one in our family circle shall be missing—so we can then be permitted to rejoice together forever.

Early in May military authorities suddenly transferred Franz to a prison in Berlin. He wrote to Francesca:

> The transfer came as a complete surprise. There was no time to take leave of comrades. . . . As far as my stand is concerned, I am still unable to come to any other decision.

The army of the Third Reich, not the Gestapo, had jurisdiction over

Franz's case. The military tribunal, scrupulously following military procedure, provided Friedrich Leo Feldmann of Dusseldorf as Franz's attorney.

Feldmann neither knew Franz nor the precise nature of his case. During his first interview Feldmann asked him to explain. Franz advised him that his refusal to serve in the army was motivated by two convictions—that Nazism was evil and causing great human suffering, and that it aimed to destroy the Catholic church. Feldmann listened respectfully, but then told him that his stand was ineffectual as far as the Nazi war machine was concerned.

Feldmann paraded before him all the familiar arguments that had been presented by the bishop of Linz, various priests, his wife and his friends. Feldmann hammered hard on Franz's statement that the Nazi regime aimed to destroy the Catholic church.

"Millions of Catholics are serving in our armed forces," he stated. "There are seminarians and priests in combat. And tell me, Franz, have any Catholic bishops called upon Catholics not to support the war or to refuse military service?"

"No," Franz replied, "I know of no such incident. But, Attorney Feldmann, I can only act on my own conscience. I do not judge anyone. I can only judge myself."

"Franz, your trial date has been set for July 6. With your attitude we don't have a chance. Please consider your family."

"Attorney Feldmann, I have considered my family. I have prayed and put myself and my family in God's hands. I know that, if I do what I think God wants me to do, he will take care of my family."

"People have told me you are a fanatic, Franz," the attorney said.

"I cannot help what people say. What do you think?"

"You are no fanatic," the lawyer responded as he rose to leave. "You still have a few days until the trial. Please, Franz, please reconsider."

Attorney Feldmann knew the trial would be a mere formality, lasting perhaps 10 minutes. He would lose the case, and Franz would lose his life. For reasons not altogether clear, he wanted very much to win the case. He realized, however, that his client's stand was hardly popular with the military, and that a noticeably spirited defense on his part could adversely affect his legal career. Nevertheless, he pursued every possible angle in his effort to defend Franz.

When Feldmann arrived at the assigned courtroom for the start of the trial, he learned that proceedings would be held up because of a hearing already in progress. Taking advantage of the delay he sought out the presiding officer of the military tribunal, introduced himself, and made an unusual request.

"Sir," he said, "I am the defense attorney for Franz Jaegerstaetter. I know that if we bring him to trial his case will be decided within minutes. I think, however, that the man deserves a little bit better than that. Would you and any other officer involved in the case be kind enough to have an informal hearing before the trial?"

"What you are asking is not done."

"I know. But would you be so kind as to consider doing it?"

Feldmann could hardly believe it when he heard the officer agree to the proposal.

As the hearing opened, the presiding judge lectured Franz with the familiar arguments.

"You are a citizen of the Third Reich. You have a duty to defend the Fatherland. We are not asking you to protect a particular regime; we are asking you to defend the Fatherland. Do you want the Russians to come into Austria to burn, loot, and rape your wife and daughters?"

Franz answered, "No."

"Well, then," the officer commanded, "defend your country!"

"I cannot. The regime is evil and I cannot support it in any way."

This is how the dialogue between the humble farmer and the powerful officers began. As it continued, Feldmann remembered, a strange dynamic occurred. The officers, who had begun imperiously, gradually softened their attitude until at the end they were pleading with Franz.

"Jaegerstaetter, we will put you in a position where you will not have to lift a gun. We will make you a medic. Please listen to us!"

"You are good men," Franz responded, "and I appreciate what you are trying to do for me. But if I join this army I feel I am doing a very bad thing, and I am adding to it the sin of lying by appearing to belong to the army by wearing its uniform. I cannot do this."

During the perfunctory trial which followed the hearing Franz was found guilty as charged with harming the war effort, and the court recom-

mended that he receive full punishment for the crime—death. Franz accepted the verdict quietly; so did Feldmann.

The attorney had lost his case but was still determined to do what he could to rescue his client. If he could persuade Franz to change his mind, he might get the court to hold off confirmation and execution of the sentence. He did two things for this purpose.

He requested that Dean Kreuzberg, a Catholic chaplain assigned to the prison, visit Franz. He hoped that Kreuzberg would persuade Franz to change his mind. The chaplain told Franz about a Pallottine priest, Father Reinisch, who had taken and stuck to the same position and who had been put to death. Knowledge that a priest had done the same thing he was doing relieved Franz of his fear that he might be following a course of action that could be considered suicide. The conversations with Father Kreuzberg did nothing to persuade him to change his mind.

Franz had decided not to inform Francesca about the trial and its outcome until the court met again to confirm the verdict and set a date for

Francesca Jaegerstaetter. From prison Franz wrote, "I still believe I can build further on your love and devotion in days to come."

the execution. He wished to keep the painful news from her until the last moment. Feldmann, however, wrote to the pastor at St. Radegund requesting that he bring Francesca to Berlin to visit her husband.

Father Furthauer brought Francesca to Berlin on Saturday of the second week of July. When they arrived at the prison, guards took them to a waiting room overlooking the prison courtyard. After some moments Francesca went to a window and looked out into the courtyard. Suddenly an army truck rolled in. A squad of soldiers jumped out of the truck and formed a circle. Then a guard threw a prisoner out of the vehicle with such force that the unfortunate man fell to the ground. Francesca recognized the prisoner immediately and screamed his name. Franz, not knowing she was in Berlin, had no idea where the voice came from and looked around wildly like a trapped animal. The soldiers dragged him to his feet and led him upstairs.

The prison authorities allowed Father Furthauer and Francesca 20 minutes for the visit. She brought Franz some food, but the guards would not let him have it. Franz gave some chocolate to Francesca for their three girls.

Both Franz's wife and pastor made last-minute attempts to change his mind. They failed. As soon as their 20 minutes had elapsed, guards terminated the meeting. Father Furthauer told Franz as he left: "You need not worry about committing a sin. You are following your own conscience and that is a good thing." The priest gave him his blessing. Francesca and Franz embraced. She turned and walked out, her heart heavy with grief.

*   *   *   *   *

During the night of August 8, 1943, Franz's cell door clanged open. A guard shoved a piece of paper at him.

"Here," he shouted, "write your last letter."

Franz addressed the letter to his wife and children:

> Along with several other men under sentence of death, I was brought into Brandenburg Prison. . . . We did not know yet what would happen to us. Not until noon was I told that my sentence was confirmed on July 14 and is to be carried out today [August 9] at 4:00 p.m. . . .

The letter did not mention that the execution would be carried out by beheading.

> . . . Dear wife and mother, I thank you once more from my heart for everything that you have done for me in my lifetime, for all the sacrifices that you have borne for me. I beg you to forgive me if I have hurt or offended you, just as I have forgiven everything. . . . It was not possible for me to free you from the pain that you must now suffer on my account. How hard it must have been for our dear Savior when, through his sufferings and death, he had to prepare such a great sorrow for his Mother, and they bore all of this out of love for us sinners.
>
> My heartfelt greetings for my dear children. I will surely beg the dear God, if I am permitted to enter heaven soon, that he will set aside a little place in heaven for all of you. In the past week I have often prayed to the Blessed Mother that, if it is God's will that I die soon, I may be permitted to celebrate the feast of the Assumption in heaven. . . .

The letter continued with various greetings to relatives and friends at St. Radegund, and then concluded:

> . . . And now your husband, son, father, son-in-law and brother-in-law greets you once more before his final journey.
> The heart of Jesus, the heart of Mary and my heart are one in time and eternity.

At the end he quoted a beautiful Austrian hymn to the Blessed Mother:

> Mary, with Child so dear, give us all your blessings.

During the evening of August 8 Father Jochmann, chaplain at Berlin's Catholic Charities Hospital, visited the cells of the condemned men. Each reacted differently to his fate. Some became desperately disoriented, crying and shouting; others screamed out their rage; still others fell into deep despair.

Father Jochmann entered Franz's cell about midnight. He had received the sacraments during the preceding afternoon, and the priest found him completely calm and prepared for death. Prison authorities had left a document on the table in the cell. He had only to sign it, and his life would be spared. Father Jochmann pointed to the paper and suggested he sign it.

"Father, I cannot do that."

The priest then offered him something to read.

Franz refused. "I am completely bound in inner union with the Lord, Father, and any reading would only interrupt that communication."

To the end of his days Father Jochmann remembered Franz's eyes shining with joy and confidence, his face full of peace.

Father Jochmann also accompanied Franz to the scaffold. The prisoner remained calm and composed. The executioner carried out the sentence.

After the execution Father Jochmann returned to the hospital. He told the nuns working there: "The military beheaded a great man. I can only congratulate you on this countryman of yours who lived as a saint and has now died a hero. I feel with certainty that this simple man is the only saint that I have ever met in my lifetime."

Franz's body was cremated at the prison in Berlin. Three years later the ashes were conveyed to St. Radegund where they were buried near a war memorial inscribed with his name and the names of nearly 60 other men from the village who had died in World War II.

*   *   *   *   *

Franz Jaegerstaetter's ashes rest in the shadow of St. Radegund's church.

On August 9, 1979, the 36th anniversary of Franz's death, Bishop Alois Wagner, auxiliary of Linz, offered a memorial Mass at St. Radegund. Francesca stands at his right.

Franz Jaegerstaetter followed his conscience to the end. Martin Luther King once said, "Cowardice asks the question, 'Is it safe?' Expediency asks the question, 'Is it politic?' Vanity asks the question, 'Is it popular?' But conscience asks the question, 'Is it right?' " Franz Jaegerstaetter's stand was not safe; it was not politic; and it was not popular. He did what he thought was right.

Acknowledgment:

A valuable source of information on the life of Franz Jaegerstaetter is *In Solitary Witness: The Life and Death of Franz Jaegerstaetter*, 1982, Liturgical Press.

Eve Lavalliere

She was sitting on a stool, elbows resting on her knees, her chin resting on her hands, watching a farmhand do the evening milking. Her large, dark eyes seemed for once to be at rest. The damp smells of the barn, the warmth of the May evening, and the silence of the French countryside all combined to create within her a feeling of tranquillity. She relished quiet moments like these; she had so few of them in her life.

Suddenly the pastor of the village, whose acquaintance she had made a few days before, strolled into the barn. As he usually did, he came directly to the point: "You, Mademoiselle, have been in my parish of Chanceaux for more than two weeks. You have not been to Mass."

Without changing position, the woman responded quietly, "Father, I have not been to Mass for years. And you have neither invited me nor given me your permission to come to your church."

"Mademoiselle, all—even sinners—are welcome in my church!"

She did not move. "I'll be there next Sunday." She said it to be rid of the priest, whom she thought slightly ridiculous.

Satisfied, the pastor turned away, strode from the barn, got on his bicycle and pedalled down the dusty road to his rectory a half-mile away. The woman continued to sit in the barn until the farmhand finished the milking.

The dialogue took place in 1917 between Father Auguste Chasteigner and Mademoiselle Eve Lavalliere, a French musical comedy actress. So lightly did Eve take the invitation that she mischievously told her companion, Leona Aumain-Delbecq, "I'll give him a bad turn or two before he finishes with me."

Father Chasteigner never did finish with Eve. It was the blasé actress who eventually did all the turning.

*   *   *   *   *

Eve Lavalliere was born Easter Sunday, April 1, 1866, in Toulon, a French port city on the Mediterranean. Her parents, Emile-Louis Fenoglio and Albanie-Marie Audonnet, christened her, their second child and first daughter, Eugenie-Marie-Pascaline. The Fenoglios had called their son, born during the first year of their marriage, Leon-Antonin.

Eugenie's problems began almost immediately. Her parents turned her over to a wet nurse who, although she loved Eugenie very much, was overly fond of wine and gave it to the baby. Eugenie developed enteritis, a painful inflamation of the intestines, which she endured till the end of her life.

Her parents, Emile, a cutter, and Albanie, a seamstress, were excellent at their trades, but they could not stitch together a good marriage. Emile, a violent man, was both an alcoholic and a libertine. He frequently beat his wife, bullied Eugenie and broke up the furniture of their humble home. Albanie and Eugenie lived in constant terror. "When he was out of the house, we worried about what condition he'd be in when he returned," Eve remembered. "When he came in, we trembled like leaves. I sat in my little chair and did not dare move." When insults and beatings were more than Albanie could bear, she would gather up the children and flee to relatives in Perpignan. "In the evening Daddy would be drunk and fighting, and Mama would run us to the railroad station," Eve recalled. "We took the train to Perpignan and would stay there until he sobered up. Then he would come and plead with Mama to come home. Mama always did,'' Eve would sigh, ''and then the whole sad business would repeat itself soon enough.''

The anguish caused by her father's violence did not pain Eugenie as much as another suffering of her early life. The little girl was fully aware that her parents did not love her. Albanie, as well as Emile, directed all her care and affection toward Leon-Antonin. ''During the evenings,'' Eve recalled, ''I had to sit in my little chair. If I dared move or open my mouth, my mother would scold me and my brother would tease me incessantly.''

When Eugenie entered a local school conducted by the Sisters of St.-Maur, her family's constant harassment led her into serious trouble. Once she broke her comb during recess. The prospect of the beating she knew she would receive when she returned home so terrorized her that she stole a comb from a schoolmate.

Uneasy, Eugenie returned home. The fragile peace of the Fenoglio household soon ruptured when the owner of the comb, her mother, and several other children pounded on the door demanding that Eugenie return the stolen article. The thief made public confession of her crime. Her outraged mother beat her before her playmates. Children and several mothers drawn into the street by the uproar applauded and cheered.

''It was,'' Eve remarked wryly in later life, ''the first public applause I ever received.''

The incident earned Eugenie the reputation of school villain. Every time anything was stolen or broken, and school authorities could not identify the person responsible, Eugenie, daughter of the frightful Fenoglio, was blamed.

The girl was hardly surprised one day when, just before school closed, the principal called her to the office and advised her that some students and teachers were accusing her of stealing ribbon from an upper-grade classroom.

''I know, Mother,'' the little girl responded, ''I heard the whispering going on all day long. Some of my friends won't even talk to me.''

''My poor child, you have borne too much suspicion and that is certainly punishment enough for you,'' the nun said.

Little Eugenie burst into tears. ''Mother, I did not steal the ribbon.''

The nun soothed her. "Don't cry, my poor little one. Just admit the crime and it will be immediately forgiven."

Confused, depressed, defeated and anxious to have the cloud disappear from over her head, Eugenie lied, "Yes, Mother, I stole the ribbon."

Armed with this confession, the principal took a piece of white cardboard and wrote on it in capital letters, T-H-I-E-F. She fastened the placard to the back of Eugenie's dress and ordered her to walk through the streets of Toulon to her home. That evening Father and Mother Fenoglio took turns whipping and cursing their wayward child.

*   *   *   *   *

A street in old Toulon, France. Eve was born here in 1866 to parents who worked in the city's famous dye and cloth industry.

Eugenie had an opportunity for a fresh start when she was 10 years old. The Fenoglios moved to Perpignan and she entered a girls' boarding school called Bon-Secours. The school, conducted by three blood sisters, the Guinards, enjoyed an excellent reputation for good teaching and discipline. Eugenie, away from the bitterness and tension of the Fenoglio home, blossomed in the cheerful atmosphere of the school.

In June of 1878 Eve's class, in preparation for first communion, made a retreat together. Rules were strict, with absolute silence at all times, even at meals, and long lectures and prayers. Eugenie, however, was never so happy. Indeed, one night near the end of her retreat, the little girl was so full of happiness and high spirits she could not contain herself. Climbing up the curtains of her little alcove in the dormitory, she straddled the metal frame from which the drapes hung. Standing atop this precarious platform, she did a few acrobatics and pantomimes. Since it was June, there was light enough for her to be seen, and the other retreatants, enthralled by the performance, giggled, laughed and clapped. Alas, the mistress of the dormitory entered. "You are all pagans," the good woman announced. "And you, Eugenie, you are an atheist." Still giggling, the "atheist" slid down the partition and into her bed and off to sleep. She knew the kind hearts of her teachers would understand her girlish exuberance, and she was right.

Eugenie's joy reached new heights the day of her first communion. Her mother had created a special dress for the occasion. "It was so beautiful," Eve remembered, "I could hardly believe she made it for me." Eugenie forgave, from her heart, her mother and father for all their unkindness to her. She experienced a rare and beautiful peace that day. It would be four decades before she would know such peace again.

*   *   *   *   *

In the late summer of 1878 Eugenie returned to her home in Perpignan. After experiencing a normal life during her stay at boarding school, she found her home situation, which had degenerated even further, absolutely intolerable. There was little, however, she could do to escape, except to do what she had done for most of her childhood—enter her fantasy world. She was determined to make these fantasies real in the world of the theater.

In a short time Eugenie, a natural leader, organized some young people in the neighborhood into a theater group. Drawing on the reservoir of fantasy she had built up over the years, Eugenie wrote plays and songs, designed sets and created costumes. Appreciative parents of her actors and actresses, including her own mother and father, formed her audiences. One of her original plays, *The Young Ladies of Normandy,* clearly revealed her talent. Actors wore Norman costumes and made many references to the Norman countryside and the idyllic beauty of its rural life. The script was pure Fenoglio fantasy. Eugenie had never been to Normandy in her life. But her rich and fertile imagination, fed by her reading, had created a story and setting that was remarkable in its detailed and accurate reproduction of the spirit and life of the region.

* * * * *

After five years in Perpignan, the Fenoglio family returned to Toulon. In 1883 Albanie, exhausted from constant domestic fighting, left her husband and returned to Perpignan. There she and Eugenie set up a household. Albanie obtained work as a seamstress and Eugenie as a dressmaker. Leon-Antonin had joined the French Navy the previous year. Emile, outraged at his wife's defection, attempted to force his way into the home at Perpignan. For once Albanie did not yield. She called the civil authorities, and they ordered her husband off the premises.

He returned to Toulon, angry and bitter. After a stretch of bad luck in gambling, Emile wheedled permission from Albanie to come for a visit. Not knowing of his gambling losses and judging that he was anxious for a reconciliation, she agreed to the visit and even prepared his favorite dishes. The naive Albanie counseled her daughter, "Be nice to your father. Make him feel at home."

Emile could not have cared less about the meals or the affection; his only concern was to squeeze money from his wife to pay off his debts.

Eve recounted the terrible events of that Sunday afternoon, March 16, 1884:

> As I waited for Daddy, I was trembling. He came, and the dinner passed at first very nice. Daddy asked me about my work and I told him how much I liked the dressmaking trade. Some musicians strolled beneath our windows to play. "There," said my father, "tell the musicians to play a little longer and throw them some money." I went to the balcony. Soon the discussion inside the house took a violent turn. I did not dare budge. Suddenly there was the sound of an explosion. I ran inside. Horror. I saw my mother falling backwards, blood on her face, and my father, with a face full of wrath and anger, turned the revolver toward me. Terror nailed me to the floor and made me mute. Then my father shrugged his shoulders as if to say, "After all, let her live."

He shot himself in the temple, and his arms fell down and he came to rest on his chair. He was dead. I called for help. People came quickly and carried me away. All that I remember besides that was how they took my mother to the hospital. My father had shot her twice in the head; one bullet had pierced her cheek but another was in deep and could not be excised. She died the 7th of April, three weeks after the day of the crime. She was 42 years old.

*   *   *   *   *

Neighbors in both Perpignan and Toulon considered the Fenoglios a bad lot. They were not loath to remind Eugenie by their harsh words and cold attitude that she was, after all, the daughter of a murderer and a suicide. Where could the 18-year-old orphan go and what could she do? Madame Garnier, a relative at Perpignan, grudgingly accepted her. Eugenie was very uncomfortable with the arrangement and left at the first opportunity. She began a series of wanderings from relative to relative, from Perpignan to Marseilles to Nice. At Nice thoughts of suicide began to plague her. She was a wanderer on the face of the earth, a lonely young woman bereft of mother and father. Even God must be against her, she felt, since she had abandoned practice of her faith. She could not seem to settle down.

One evening Eugenie sat in front of a deep stream in Nice, head in hands, looking at the water. Hours passed. It grew dark. A gentleman passing by noticed her and walked quietly over to her.

"Little one, have you had any supper?"

She turned her beautiful face to him. It was full of sadness and fear. "No sir, I have not."

"Come with me."

The gentleman took her to supper and arranged for a night's lodging. The next day he met with her and, perhaps as a result of their conversations, arranged for her to meet the director of a traveling theatrical group. The director, a friend of his, accepted Eugenie as a member of the group. It was the start of her slow rise to stardom.

For three years Eugenie traveled through the Mediterranean coastal 'cities of France learning the theatrical trade. The director, an honest and good man, kept a paternal and protective eye on the young ladies in the troupe. He hired female chaperones to watch over them, for he knew they were subject to serious temptations. Eugenie was no exception. Pert, pixie-like, attractive, she drew an enthusiastic response from the men in the audiences.

A certain Marquis de la Valette, taking advantage of the director's absence one evening, convinced Eugenie he admired her so much that he would be delighted to set her up in her own apartment with a maid, jewelry, furs, and everything else she might want. The girl's head swam with the prospect, and she accepted his offer. It wasn't long afterward that the marquis demanded and received from Eugenie what he really wanted.

One of Eugenie's relatives in Perpignan, meanwhile, listed her as a missing person and the police began to investigate her disappearance. The marquis, hearing the news, panicked. He knew he could be jailed for corrupting a minor. He persuaded Eugenie to change her name. She did so, calling herself Eve Lavalliere. She loved the sound of the name; it was famous in French history as the name of the mistress of Louis XIV, a woman who spent her last days doing penance as a Carmelite nun. The resourceful marquis also suggested that Eve, to avoid police detection, wear men's clothes when leaving and entering the apartment.

After some time Eve grew bored with both the provincial theater circuit and her aging marquis. She felt she had served her apprenticeship and

"Paris' most Parisian comedienne. She is a symbol of the city, witty, elegant, enigmatic, audacious."

was ready to try to win fame in Paris. The fledgling actress, however, did not leave the circuit in haste. She saved all the money she could over a period of several months and arranged for interviews in Paris. Then she quietly packed her best furs and dresses and in the company of her servant, Celestine, left her marquis without even saying *au revoir*!

*   *   *   *   *

Immediately upon arriving in Paris the 22-year-old Mademoiselle Lavalliere began studies under the city's finest theatrical coach, a man of such excellent character that people in show business called him "Father" Dulaurens. He began Eve's lessons in diction, singing and dancing. After several months of primary training, Dulaurens obtained a job for her in the chorus line of the Varietes, a musical comedy theater, at a starting salary of 45 francs a month. Although Mr. Bertrand, the director of the Varietes, recognized her potential, it took Eve more than 10 years of drudgery before she achieved stardom. It might have taken longer had she not met Fernand Samuel.

Parisians called him "Samuel the Magnificent," and the entire city idolized him. "The Magnificent," a man of intelligence, imagination and finesse, enjoyed a reputation for integrity and honesty in the theatrical business. He assumed directorship of the Varietes in 1892 and took Eve under his personal tutelage. He supervised her long hours of training, inspired her to discipline her raw and uneven talent, and gradually shaped her into a star that shone brilliantly on the Parisian stage for 17 seasons. Samuel knew exactly the nature of Eve's genius; she was a born comedienne rather than a dramatic actress. Samuel bent his immense energy to smoothing and polishing the rough diamond of her talent.

He fell in love with her, and she with him. In 1895 Eve bore him a daughter. Although she had given up the practice of her faith, and Samuel's practice was erratic, they had the child baptized. Only St. Peter's in Rome suited Samuel for the baptism, so the baby was baptized there and given the name Jeanne.

There was no denying Eve and Samuel's devotion to each other. Unfortunately, Samuel was devoted to several other women as well, and they to

Paris' Varieties Theatre in 1904. Eve had already achieved stardom here and was to remain the main attraction for 13 more years.

him. When Eve discovered his philandering in 1897, she broke off the affair. It was another bitter experience for her. Samuel was the only man she ever truly loved. "He did me too much good and too much bad for me to ever forget him," she later remarked. "The bad came from his vices, the good from his generous heart." The two continued to work together professionally, maintaining a mutual respect and even tenderness toward each other.

*   *   *   *   *

Eve lived well in Paris. Her many wealthy gentlemen friends were more than willing to supplement her meager salary. Apart from Samuel, Eve's sole basis for a relationship with any man was the amount of money he could provide her. Her group of admirers included business magnates, statesmen and royalty. She was as reckless and restless with these men as she was in every area of her life away from the stage.

Her longest liaison was with the German aspirin millionaire, Baron Georg von Lucius. Von Lucius, madly in love with her, called the "divine Eve" as much a part of Paris as the Champs Elysées. The baron, married and a member of the German diplomatic corps in Paris, took up with Eve after her episode with Samuel.

While the two of them were sightseeing in the great cathedral at Chartres one day, Georg wrung from Eve a promise to marry him as soon as he could free himself from his existing marital responsibilities. Once outside the great cathedral, however, Eve advised him, "I will not marry you."

"How can you make so light of your promises?" the outraged diplomat cried.

"How could I help it?" she replied. "We were in that magnificent monument and you were crying out like a cow."

After World War I broke out in 1914, the German government posted von Lucius to its embassy at Stockholm, Sweden. Eve and the baron stayed in touch by mail. In one letter, written shortly after he was appointed a counselor there, Eve wrote:

> Bravo, I was delighted to hear about your appointment as
> Counselor. It certainly took them long enough to give you
> this honor. You, a Counselor—one who gives counsel.

Fernand Samuel, Eve's mentor and the father of her daughter, Jeanne, was the only man Eve ever truly loved. They continued to work together professionally after their personal relationship had foundered.

I am going to Versailles on the first of June and I plan to stay there for the whole month. Please do not forget my one thousand francs, as I want to make some gifts and I have several bills to pay. As you know, I will be staying at the villa which, because it has gas and electricity, will cost twice as much.

But, enough of this dirty question of money. I am embarrassed to even mention it, my gentle Counselor, whom I love with all my heart.

Eve

P.S. I love you very much. You are a fascinating man. Please do not forget my check.

She often spoke of the poor baron as "the most boring man in the world. I never look at him without getting sick, but he certainly is a generous and convenient banker."

*   *   *   *   *

Eve had bottom billing on the Varietes posters in 1892. As the years went on and her training and experience progressed, however, she earned more important roles. By 1900 she acquired top billing and began to lead the Varietes theater into a golden age. Behind the whole success story was Samuel. He had assembled a group of writers, musicians and artists, and had tailored their efforts to Eve's special talents. Newspapers called his organization "The Iron Troupe" because of its unbroken series of successes.

"They own the boulevards, they own Paris, they own the world," one French critic wrote enthusiastically. "Lavalliere is an exquisite animal," another exclaimed. The little Fenoglio girl, with her bobbed hair, chic figure, insouciant manner and spontaneity, electrified her audiences. Crowned heads of Europe made special trips to Paris to see her perform. The prestigious Academie Francais invited her to demonstrate the tango, the latest dance rage.

An American journalist writing in *Harper's Bazaar* in 1914 typified the frustrations newspapermen experienced as they attempted to describe her. Having made an appointment for an interview in her dressing room, he waited for her to finish a performance.

> Presently, she came in. I was going to say she floated in, but she didn't. She didn't even glide. Nor did she frou-frou (rustle). Before I realized it, she was shaking hands with me, both hands as if I were a long-lost brother. "I am learning English," she said.

She bewitched English and American theater critics. "She is the liveliest thing I have seen in many a long day," exulted the *Chicago Examiner*'s critic in 1906. He went on to say, "She is always in a series of paroxysmal gestures—never still for a moment."

Gertrude Norman, an English newspaperwoman, described her as "Paris' most Parisian comedienne. She is a symbol of the city—witty, elegant, enigmatic, audacious."

In a lengthy article in the August 1911 issue of the British magazine, *Theatre,* Norman analyzed the genius of Lavalliere:

> She possesses the careless, laughing wit of the Parisian cafes, the ever-ready repartee, the graceful mode of thought and expression, the merry disposition with its contradiction of quick pathos and neurotic charm. . . . Lavalliere is slender, small, light, full of a curious alert, definite grace. She possesses a precision of abandonment which is almost boyish in its air of impertinent daring. Her most noticeable quality, even more so than her beautiful eyes . . . is the exceptional beauty of her speaking voice. . . .

Norman unwittingly became a prophet:

> She has the eyes of a nun; the voice of an ecstatic . . . her diction is superb.

The writer continued:

> What is most remarkable about Eve Lavalliere is her hands. Just by using her hands, Lavalliere keeps the theater in an uproar of laughter. She uses her thumb alone as a sculptor or painter uses a chisel or brush.

Another analyst of Lavalliere's genius pointed out that she used her hands

> . . . not so much as a graceful or pretty movement, as a movement which symbolizes well her imaginative powers and the will power to create with her hands what she imagines in her mind.

On the Parisian stage Eve fully expressed in her eyes, her mouth and with her hands the fantasy life she had begun to live so many years earlier.

*   *   *   *   *

Fame, success and riches left Eve cold. The only time she enjoyed any peace within herself was on the stage. "I never enjoy myself, anywhere," she confided to a friend. "I always withdraw into myself wherever I am, except when I am on the stage."

Her large, shining black eyes mirrored the insuperable melancholy that filled her heart. She found no comfort in relationships with men, nor in her daughter who disliked her and whom Samuel had thoroughly spoiled.

Thoughts of suicide haunted her again and again. She claimed to have actually attempted to kill herself three times.

Once, after returning from a successful Red Cross drive in England, she attended a dinner party at an opulent French chateau. During the evening's dancing she slipped out and entered the woods surrounding the chateau. She found a stream and once more considered drowning herself. Suddenly a cigarette glowed in the dark. Eve hid and after regaining her composure walked back through the woods and into the grand salon. No one had noticed her absence, and her smiling face belied the terrible sense of despair she was experiencing in her heart.

Another time, after a particularly brilliant performance, she exited through the theater's back door and, alone, walked through the streets of Paris until she came to the banks of the River Seine. She bent over the waters and looked into them as a source of relief from her inner sufferings. A tap on her shoulder broke her melancholy reverie.

"Madame, can I help?" The speaker, an older man, was obviously a common laborer.

"Thank you very much, but I do not think so," she replied.

The man peered at her closely in the dark. "My God, you are Eve Lavalliere," he exclaimed.

"How do you know that?" the trembling Eve inquired.

"Mademoiselle Lavalliere, I am one of your greatest fans. Come, come now, let us walk home together."

With true French delicacy, the gentleman never told this story to anyone. It was Eve herself who recounted it.

She also revealed to Leona, the Belgian orphan who became her companion in 1915, that on a third occasion she went into her bedroom and attempted suicide but lost her nerve at the last moment.

* * * * *

At a rehearsal in 1911 a coil of heavy rope fell from the upper reaches of the stage and struck Eve on the head. She was hospitalized and required surgery. During her stay in the hospital, she told one of the nuns: "I am not afraid of death, Sister. I am afraid of life.'' During this illness she saw a priest, but it is doubtful that she ever received the sacraments.

In any event, if there were any religious conversion on her part, it was short-lived. On her return to the theater, she resumed her former lifestyle.

When Samuel died in 1914, Eve suffered a severe depression. The critics noticed. ''In her eyes of fire,'' one wrote, ''there is a note of sadness. One feels her soul is burning.''

Eve had hoped, with Samuel's demise, that relations with her daughter might improve. Her hopes were in vain. The girl had taken to wearing men's clothing and openly flaunted her female companions before her mother.

World War I broke out in August 1914. As the French war effort escalated, Eve performed benefit after benefit for the troops. She journeyed through France and England raising funds for the war effort and visiting the wounded. She was near physical and mental exhaustion. Thoughts of suicide persisted. But, trouper that she was, she continued to perform.

In January 1915 the American show-business magazine, *Variety,* noted:

> Two thousand dollars is the price set by Lavalliere, a noted French actress, to appear in American vaudeville in an English-speaking sketch. H. B. Marinelli received a cable this week giving this information. He cabled back asking how many people Lavalliere would bring over, believing the managers for that price nowadays would expect the French Right Wing.

In May 1917 negotiations were concluded for an American tour, and she signed a lucrative contract. She was to tour the United States in the fall of 1917.

Eve decided to spend the summer of that year in the quiet French countryside, resting and studying the script for the American tour. She took her servants and a young companion, Leona, to Chanceaux-sur-Choiselle and rented a handsome chateau there with the unhandsome name, The Piggery. Father Chasteigner, the village priest, was the agent for the French family who owned the chateau; it was with him that Eve negotiated the contract for the summer rental.

Father Chasteigner, 52 at the time, was of peasant stock. Tall, broad, he possessed a loud voice, florid complexion, clear eyes and a delightful sense of humor. He was fond of the district's good wine. "He not only drinks it at Mass," gossipy parishioners commented, "but also at Vespers and the ringing of the Angelus." Compassionate, faithful to his word, honest, Father Chasteigner was a good priest and a thoroughly good human being.

Although Father Chasteigner had put her nose slightly out of joint, Eve did accept his invitation and attended Mass with Leona on June 3. The two sat right under the pulpit. The pastor, not known for his subtlety, shouted his sermon right at the two women. The topic was "The Great Conversions of History." Eve left after Mass, furious for having to endure the silly ordeal. In the afternoon when she had simmered down, lo and behold, up the dusty road bicycled the pastor.

"How did you like my sermon, Mademoiselle? I prepared it especially for you."

"Really," Eve responded coldly.

"You enjoyed it?"

"Father, you do not know how to preach; you shout!"

"Mademoiselle?" Now it was the pastor's turn to suffer as he endured a lesson in diction from the great Lavalliere herself.

"Mademoiselle, you are speaking only of form. The substance of my

Leona Aumain-Delbecq, a Belgian war orphan, became Eve's companion in 1915.

sermon does not concern you. . . ." His voice grew louder, his temper began to boil. "I would not suffer anyone else but you to lecture me on preaching!" With that, he got on his bicycle and pedalled back to his rectory to nurse his wounded ego.

The next day Father Chasteigner, slightly chastened, pedalled out again to visit Eve. "Come, join me for a walk," the priest suggested. Because both of them were still smarting from the spirited exchange of the preceding day, they could do little else except engage in small talk. Father Chasteigner, who was not made for tiptoeing around anything, soon exhausted his small store of patience. "What a pity you do not have the faith," he observed candidly.

Eve glared at him. "Faith, faith! What good is faith?" she countered. "My experience with faith has all been bad. It is not, Father, that I do not believe in another world; I have tried with many of my friends and famous people in Paris to reach the other world. We practiced spiritualism. We were under the direction of a woman medium who had direct contact with Lucifer."

Father Chasteigner could not believe his ears. His temper began to rise again.

"I wanted to stay young," Eve continued. "I wanted 20 more years of youth and I asked the devil for it. He responded by knocking on the table. Later on, he actually appeared at the seance. . . . I made a deal with him for health and preservation of my youth in exchange for the many recruits I would bring. The devil did not restore my health. I am still growing older. I finally told the medium that spiritualism was a fraud and that there are no devils."

Father Chasteigner was appalled. "What did you say? There are no devils? Mademoiselle, there are devils. You had better stop this spiritualism nonsense. The next time you may not be so fortunate." Once again his temper blazed and, with a "Goodbye Mademoiselle," he mounted his bicycle and pedalled down the dusty road as if the devil were at his back.

Eve watched the priest disappear in the dust. As her eyes followed him, her mind worked furiously. "He's right, there is a devil. And, if there is a devil, there must be a God. And, if there is a God, what am I doing on earth? What am I doing with the life he gave me?"

Eve admitted later that this was the decisive moment of her conversion. "It was because of the devil," she remarked dryly, "that I came to God."

The pastor appeared again the following day. Leona remembered that Eve's attitude toward him was "more deferential, quiet and serious."

"You threw me for a loop yesterday, Mademoiselle," the priest said. "I was really shaken and spent a good part of the evening on my knees trying to ask God to help me to help you. I don't know what to do. I offered Mass for your intentions this morning." And then, as subtle as usual, he handed Eve the *Life of Mary Magdalen* by Father Lacordaire. "Read this book on your knees," he said. "Let's see what the good God can do for a woman like you."

After lunch Eve read the book aloud to Leona. Leona, who had heard Eve act on the stage, recalled: "I never heard her speak with so much emotion. The reading was punctuated by genuine sobbing." Grace had touched her heart.

Soon Father Chasteigner bicycled back again. "Come," he said to Eve, "let's take a walk."

As they strolled around the tree-lined avenues surrounding the chateau, Eve told him Leona would like to make her first communion. "Can I help in instructing her?" Eve inquired.

"What?" the priest said.

"Yes, I know I am a sinner and I know I haven't been living like a Christian, but I am hoping that God will permit me to return to him and take communion with Leona." As Eve spoke about returning to the practice of the faith, the priest's steps grew longer and faster. Tiny Eve found herself running beside him. She began to yell. Leona recalled: "I never heard her speak with such fire."

Eve began to accuse herself of all her faults. Father Chasteigner was embarrassed. "Wait a little bit, Mademoiselle," he said, "you cannot cry out like that."

"Wait!" she answered. "Why should I wait? Can't I share in Leona's happiness?"

"Leona is only a child compared to you. You are Eve Lavalliere. You are well-known. Your life is more public. I can't treat it in the same way and, besides, you have fooled around with spiritualism. That's a reserved sin. I have to get permission from the archbishop to give you absolution.''

"O my God, why am I so miserable? You do not wish to do anything for me. The good God doesn't wish to do anything for me. What is going to become of me?''

"Oh, calm down,'' the priest replied. "I know God loves you. He always does. And, just to prove how he uses people like me to show his love, I'm getting on my bicycle right now and going to Tours to get the necessary permission for absolution.''

"Go quickly, I beg you,'' Eve pleaded.

"I'm running,'' he answered. "I'll be back in an hour. Watch the road. As soon as I come into sight, if I have the permission, I will wave my beret.''

Leona recalled that as one of the most terrible hours of Eve's life. "She walked up and down the road. She cried. She wept, complained, wrung her hands.'' It was Lavalliere at her best, but this time the actress wasn't acting. As the hour passed slowly, Eve grew ever more agitated. She got on her knees, and Leona remembered her lifting her arms to heaven, crying out to God to take her. She could not stand the terrible wait. Suddenly the figure of Father Chasteigner, pedalling with all his might, came into view. He was waving his beret wildly in the air. The pastor was ready to bring Eve Lavalliere home.

On June 18, 1917, Leona and Eve received communion from Father Chasteigner in the parish church of Chanceaux. His emotion was so strong that his hands trembled as he gave the sacred host to Eve.

*   *   *   *   *

Father Chasteigner was surprised when Eve rejected his suggestion in the fall of 1917 that she return to the stage. "You can be a good actress and a good Christian as well,'' he advised.

"No, Father, I have made up my mind. I will never return to the theater.'' She contacted the promoters of the American tour, cancelled her contract, and offered appropriate conpensation to the managers of the project.

Eve, in the first blush of conversion, determined to enter a Carmelite cloister. Father Chasteigner, aware of her fragile health and restless disposition, advised against it. Eve and Leona settled in Lourdes in November. During this time Eve decided to give up the use of makeup and hair dye. It was a decision she agonized over for weeks.

Despite the priest's advice, Eve continued in her attempts to enter a Carmelite cloister. She tried several convents, but each one turned her down. Carmelite authorities knew her health was poor and feared the glare of publicity that would focus on the quiet cloisters if Eve entered.

Angry with God because of the rejections, Eve grew more and more depressed. It was some days before she realized that the good Lord was permitting her to experience the bitterness of rejection, the same rejection suffered by the Son.

In March 1918 she returned to Paris. She sold her two apartments, the one in the city and the other at Auteuil. She liquidated all the artworks, furnishings and books. She gave the money realized from these transactions to the poor. While in the city she met many former show-business acquaintances. She had changed so much in manner and dress, however, that they hardly recognized her. The only trademark that survived her crisis was her eyes, still luminous and dark but now filled with peace. Many of her friends burst into tears when they met her. They simply could not understand what had gone on within the complicated heart of Eve Lavalliere.

Eve retired from the stage—still very much in demand—at the age of 51.

No one could understand her disappearance. The press attributed the wildest motives to her. Rumors had it that she had murdered someone, that a young man had threatened to kill himself and her, that she had never recovered from Samuel's death. But the wildest of all gossip held that she had been involved in espionage. The French secret police actually did suspect her of this crime and summoned her to answer charges. "You were in contact with Baron von Lucius, formerly a member of the German Embassy in Paris. He is now in Stockholm, and we know that he has been sending you money." Eve acknowledged that she had received money from the baron all during the war, but told the police also that she had used it to support her two apartments and by this time had ended contact with him.

This notoriety aggravated her. Her enteritis continued to plague her, along with stomach and kidney disorders. Despite all this she continued to fly like a restless bird throughout the country. In 1918 she left Lourdes because of troublesome publicity and poor health. She went from there to Paris, to St.-Baslemont, back to Chanceaux, then again to Lourdes. The following year she lighted in no less than eight different places. A nun remarked: "Eve, you are going through your purgatory with your suitcase in hand."

She attempted to reconcile herself with her daughter, but without success. Jeanne continued to flaunt her lifestyle before her mother. Eve suffered yet another bitter rejection when one of Jeanne's female companions forced the former actress, with Jeanne's consent, to leave the St.-Baslemont chateau that had been willed to Jeanne by her father.

Through the efforts of Father Chasteigner, Eve finally found a small home in Thuillieres in Vosges, a quiet province of France. Leona and Eve settled there in September 1920 and, in honor of Martha and Mary's home, called their new house Bethany.

In her spiritual notebook Eve wrote:

Bethany is a house consecrated and given to the Sacred Heart
by the hands of the Divine Mother. I thank you, O my God,
that you have given me shelter beneath your roof. Abandon-
ment, love, trust—such is my motto. O Sacred Heart of
Jesus, may your kingdom come. My Lord and my God.

Eve was idyllically happy. "In this lost corner of Lorraine, far from the world, we will tarry for God's will in stillness and meditation," she wrote.

She took an active role in her parish, organizing the children's choir. Under her direction the little ones added much beauty to church services and liturgies. As happens in parishes, however, a group complained about her. Rather than cause difficulty, she ceased her work. Eve was deeply hurt by this, another rejection.

In the same year she joined the Third Order Secular of St. Francis, taking the name Sister Eve Marie of the Sacred Heart of Jesus.

The Franciscan spirit—missionary zeal, love of poverty, admiration of nature, devotion to the gospel and union with Christ crucified in sufferings—deeply influenced the last years of Eve's life.

Despite ill health Eve desired to serve the church's missionary efforts.

Eve (*second from left, front row*) as a lay missionary in North Africa. "You are going to help this mission," Archbishop Lemaitre told her, "not by your deeds, but by your suffering."

While in Lourdes in 1917 she had met Archbishop Lemaitre of Carthage. The missionary was developing a lay missionary organization to serve sick Arab children in his extensive and impoverished territory. From November 1921 to 1924, Eve spent seven months each year in Tunisia as a member of a nursing team. Unfortunately, she was never too effective because her own health was so poor. In 1924 the archbishop advised her not to return the next winter. "You are going to help this mission, Mademoiselle, not by your deeds, but by your sufferings," he told her. "Your task has just begun. Thanks to your sacrifices, this mission will prosper."

Back home again in November 1924 Eve resumed a daily schedule of prayer, good works, spiritual reading, meals and meditation with Leona. Eve filled page after page of her notebook with clear, candid and unpretentious spiritual reflections. She wrote to Father Chasteigner, "My physical health and my spiritual health are being maintained. Praise be to God who is their author." She also wrote a letter of love and gratitude to "My Jesus" which revealed the ardor of her love and the complete consecration of herself as a penitent to the will of God. She was dead to the world and dead to herself so that Jesus alone might reign within her. "It is through suffering," Eve wrote, "that we most resemble Jesus."

In August 1928 Eve entered into the last stations of her way of the cross. She suffered a severe bout of peritonitis. Doctor Grosjean, her physician, ordered her to bed. She ran severe temperatures and experienced great pain. Jeanne, her daughter, came from St.-Baslemont to assist Leona in caring for her. One evening, when Jeanne and Eve were alone, the girl placed a knife blade under her mother's nose. On the blade was a white powder. "Sniff this, Mother," Jeanne said. "It will do you good." Eve did as commanded; afterward she felt better and was able to sleep. No wonder. The white powder was cocaine. Jeanne, short on funds, was attempting to hook her mother on the drug. Once Eve was dependent, her daughter would sell her all she needed. It was eight days before the physician discovered Jeanne's "treatment." When he did, he personally threw her out of the house. Because of Eve's addiction, Dr. Grosjean had to keep her on a maintenance dose of the drug until her death a year and a half later.

That year and a half was marked by intense suffering. Eve's face swelled beyond recognition. Her teeth fell out. Her mouth became a mass of

Eve's funeral procession moved quietly through the lanes of the village of Thuillieres.

swollen tissue. The doctor had to sew her eyelids together; her once beautiful eyes were hidden. As each of her once beautiful features sustained attack, Eve gave thanks to God. "I have sinned through these faculties, good Lord. Now I thank you for permitting me to expiate my sins through this suffering."

In her agony she still thought of others. She sent a gift of an old theater program to Father Chasteigner and prayed that Leona would find a good Christian husband. Leona did, and that brought great joy to Eve.

On Wednesday, July 10, 1929, Eugenie-Marie Fenoglio, Eve Lavalliere, Sister Eve Marie of the Sacred Heart of Jesus, died. At the end the priest said to her, "God has pardoned you because you have loved much. Depart in peace, O liberated Christian soul."

Eve wrote her own epitaph in a notebook a short time before her death: "My Maker, have mercy."

Eve Lavalliere is buried by the tiny church in Thullieres.
Eugenie-Marie Fenoglio, Eve Lavalliere, Sister Eve Marie
found rest in the promise of eternal life.

Titus Brandsma

"Anno, do you know what?"

"What, Father?"

"You are a very bright boy!"

The speaker was a Dutch Franciscan friar; the bright young man, a student at the Franciscan minor seminary in Megen, the Netherlands.

"You are too bright to be a Franciscan," the priest continued.

"There are many bright Franciscans, Father."

"I am talking about you, Anno. You should be a Jesuit . . . not a Franciscan."

This conversation took place just before the turn of the 20th century. And, as happens in every century, the young man took none of his elder's advice. He joined neither the Franciscans nor the Jesuits; he became a Carmelite priest. His name was Anno Sjoerd Brandsma. He was born in Friesland, a province in the northwest corner of the Netherlands on February 23, 1881.

Anno's ancestors scooped their land from the sea, first with bare hands and later with primitive tools. Living with their faces to the sea and

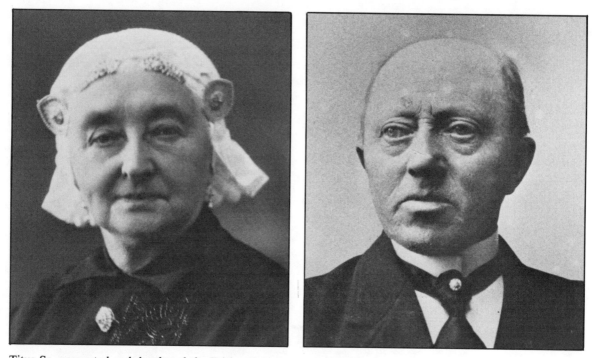

Titus Sr. promoted and developed the Frisian dairy cooperative and was active in local politics. With his wife, Tjitsje, they raised six children.

their feet on fertile farmland wrested from the waters, the Frisians were—and are—an enterprising and quietly determined people, a distinct and colorful minority in the densely populated Netherlands. Physically strong, they revere decency of life and foster all the qualities that have made the Dutch famous—cleanliness, order, intelligence and discipline.

Anno's father, Titus, a sober and creative man, deeply loved his people and his Catholic faith. He promoted and developed the Frisian cooperative dairy system and immersed himself in local politics. He and his wife, Tjitsje Postma, had six children, four girls and two boys, whom they reared in an atmosphere of piety, hard work and joy on the large farm they called Oegeklooster. The family attended daily Mass and contrary to the custom of the times, Titus and Tjitsje received communion frequently during the week. Titus loved music and frequently gathered his brood around the family piano for sing-a-longs and dancing lessons. An accomplished folk dancer, farmer Brandsma enlivened many of his family's happiest hours as he taught his children the steps of intricate polkas and mazurkas.

*   *   *   *   *

Anno desired to become a priest from the time he was a young boy. At the age of 11, he asked his father's permission to enter the Franciscan minor seminary in Megen to begin preparatory studies. He was a frail boy and not blessed with the strong constitution typical of his people. He was a willing worker but could never handle the heavy farm work Frisian children customarily performed. Titus and Tjitsje, although concerned about his health, gave him permission to try the seminary, and Anno left home in the fall of 1892.

During his six years at Megen, Anno, well-endowed with Frisian common sense and stability and possessed of keen intelligence, succeeded very well in his studies. His winsome personality made him a favorite with professors and students. His classmates called him ''de Punt,'' a nickname meaning ''Shorty.'' In his third year at the seminary he developed a severe

The Brandsmas raised their family in an atmosphere of piety, hard work and joy. Anno is at the far left.

Located in Friesland near the North Sea, the farmhouse was the pride of the Brandsma family.

intestinal disorder and lost a considerable amount of weight. The friars ordered a special diet for him, featuring cream, eggs, butter and other foods that enabled him to regain his lost weight. He soon recovered his health and returned with renewed energies to his studies. His superiors, however, not satisfied that he was strong enough for the rigors of Dutch Franciscan life, suggested that he seek a gentler form of life. The rejection hurt, but Anno accepted it with grace and resiliency.

In September 1898, Anno presented himself at the Carmelite monastery in Boxmeer, Holland, as a candidate for the order and was cheerfully accepted. On entering the novitiate he observed the custom of changing his name to indicate the beginning of his new life. His choice was Titus.

Carmelites trace their origin to Holy Land pilgrims and ex-crusaders who, in the spirit of the Old Testament prophet Elias, adopted an eremitical form of life on and around Mt. Carmel about the middle of the 12th century. Their primitive rule was approved by Pope Honorius III in 1226. Twenty-one years later St. Simon Stock, to whom Mary revealed the scapular, became general superior of the order and the strong leader of its establishment and spread in Europe.

Despite internal divisions and vagaries of religious and political revolutions, the Carmelites contributed significantly to the ministry of the church in Europe until the 18th century when the order fell afoul of the Austrian emperor's anti-papal policies and the atheism unleashed by French revolutionaries. By 1830 there were only two Carmelite monasteries in western Europe: one in Austria with three members and the other in Boxmeer with three members.

A decade later the Boxmeer community, freed from the political oppression that had been suffocating it, attracted new members and stirred with new life. By the 1850s the community had 24 members and began sending men on mission to pioneer the foundation of new monasteries in the Netherlands, England, the United States, Poland, France and Austria. Carmelites from Boxmeer eventually opened missions in Brazil and Indonesia.

Anno joined the Carmelites as this wave of renewal was cresting. The Boxmeer community consisted of 39 friars who spent their days in prayer, silence and solitude. Fasting, austerity, contemplation and study were the

His parents delighted in young Anno's scholastic achievements.

ingredients of the Carmelite way. Anno—living in a simple cell, sleeping on a straw mattress, bending over books at his desk, kneeling in quiet prayer, chanting the midnight office in the chapel, eating the simplest foods, recreating quietly with his confreres—knew he had found his niche. "I am very happy now," he wrote home.

During his novitiate, Titus began a lifelong study of the writings of St. Teresa of Avila, the most astute and articulate analyst of the Carmelite spirit. (In 1970 Teresa was proclaimed a Doctor of the Church.) In his spare time, he translated several of her works and published them in 1901 under the title, *Selected Writings From the Works of St. Teresa.* The effort represented the first of his many contributions to the literature of mysticism. He discovered that he had a facile pen and an ability to translate the most scholarly concepts into clear, concise language. These translations marked the beginning of a long and successful literary career.

Titus also initiated several literary projects with his fellow students during his novitiate and subsequent years of study. He encouraged them to produce articles on various religious topics and acted as their literary agent in selling their work to Dutch magazines and newspapers. He developed an in-house magazine for the Carmelites which he eventually published for all Dutch Catholics. These early writings revealed his characteristically Carmelite attraction to mysticism and his typically Frisian interest in Christian responsibility for social justice.

At times his austere lifestyle, coupled with the added exertions of translating and writing, took a heavy toll on Titus' fragile constitution. He experienced recurrent attacks of intestinal difficulties and general weakness. His superior, a gentle and sensible Dutchman, often grounded him, relieving him of the obligation to assist at midnight office and other monastic duties. The friars, anxious that Titus stay in their community, assisted him in every possible manner.

His courage did not flag. On one occasion he wrote to his grandmother, who was also probably ill at the time: "Keep up your courage and continue to be happy. Then everything will right itself. . . . Do believe this."

In October 1899, his Carmelite superiors allowed their happy, if frail, Titus to profess his first vows in the order and approved the continuation of his studies for the priesthood.

Bright and articulate, Titus had little difficulty in mastering the re-

Five of the six Brandsma children entered religious life.

quired studies in philosophy and theology. He was ordained a priest June 17, 1905, celebrated his first solemn Mass in Friesland and, after a short vacation with parents and relatives, reported to the Carmelite monastery in Oss for his final year of theology.

His superiors intended to send Titus to Rome for doctoral studies. During final examinations at Oss, however, he ran afoul of a testy examining professor who resented his liberal thinking, picked him to shreds in oral questioning, and effectively squelched for the time being any hope for studies in the Eternal City. Titus, while accepting this setback with some degree of resignation, was jolted again when his superiors assigned him, a respected scholar and successful writer, to sacristan and bookkeeping duties at Boxmeer. Always resilient, the new priest graciously and cheerfully accepted the assignment.

The appointment to Rome for doctoral studies came a year later, after his superiors judged they could override the objections of the professor who had previously flunked him.

Titus' calmness, gentleness and quiet good humor won him the affection and admiration of the international group of students at the Carmelite College of St. Albert in Rome. Illness plagued him again, however, preventing him from passing final examinations the first time. After a successful second try, he was awarded a doctorate in philosophy by the Pontifical Gregorian University October 25, 1909.

*   *   *   *   *

Titus, a doctor of philosophy, returned to the Netherlands to assume a teaching post at Oss.

Carmelite renewal had peaked during the early 1900s but, by the time of his return from Rome, vocations to his and other orders had dropped sharply. He nevertheless labored to establish the best training system possible for the small number of seminarians. Superiors of the order, responding to the urgings of Titus and other scholars, determined to provide the most competent faculties and the finest seminary programs. During some terms Titus taught only two or three students, always with well-prepared and thoroughly researched lectures and classes. His subject matter dealt with the relationship between philosophy and theology.

Titus combined writing and other activities with his teaching career. He founded *Carmelrozen,* a journal of Carmelite spirituality, which he edited and for which he encouraged his students to write. In 1916 he organized a team of scholars to do more translations of the voluminous works of St. Teresa of Avila. He was appointed editor of the local daily newspaper in 1919 and collaborated on a Frisian translation of the famous spiritual guide, *Imitation of Christ.* Ever the practical businessman, he negotiated government and business loans for a new library in Oss and engaged in numerous civic and religious projects.

Despite his time-consuming round of activities, Titus never neglected his Carmelite way of life, which demanded several hours of prayer and meditation each day. No wonder he wrote to a friend: "Last night I was still working until one-thirty, and this morning I said Mass at six-thirty since school started again at eight o'clock.'' No wonder also that from time to time his health broke under the strain.

His spirit was willing but his flesh was too weak to maintain the fast and demanding pace of his apostolic involvements. In the summer of 1921 he suffered a general physical collapse and, with recurrent hemorrhaging and persistent pain, hovered between life and death for many weeks. Then, suddenly Titus began to recover and was back to full stride by early winter of that year.

*   *   *   *   *

Busy Titus always had time for people. The more unfortunate they were, the more time he gave them. The eccentric, the poor, the ignorant, the despised—all felt at home with him and had no hesitation about invading his privacy. His heart, overuling his fondness for organizatin, impelled him to drop everything and turn full attention to the plight of any distressed person who showed up, unannounced, at his doorstep. When he met people who were hungry, he fed them. If he had no money to give, he brought them to his home. He provided clothing, rent, money and consolation without stint to all who came his way. Once he took the blanket off his own bed to warm a poor person. He spent hours listening to the complaints of frustrated artists and outraged scholars, and struggled to right the wrongs they suffered. If his head was in the high and luminous clouds of philosophy and mysticism, his feet were planted firmly on the rocky ground of human suffering and confusion.

Kneeling in prayer by the hour, leaning over his desk while preparing his lectures, listening patiently to the words of a suffering human being, counseling a student, sitting at his typewriter with his head concealed by billows of blue smoke from the cigar clenched in his teeth—Titus Brandsma was a happy man. And he brought happiness with everything he did and to everyone he met.

*   *   *   *   *

In 1929 Father Brandsma supervised the completion of a Carmelite
monastery in Nijmegen.

The Catholic University of Nijmegen, the first of its kind in the
modern history of the Netherlands, was established in 1923. It symbolized
the endurance and hardiness of Dutch Catholics who had suffered severe
persecution during several centuries of political and religious upheaval, and
were still struggling for survival and equality in the 20th century.

Dutch Protestants and Catholics took religion seriously. Both were
quite willing to die for their beliefs, and since the Reformation each provided
the opportunity for the other to do so at various intervals. By the end of the
19th century, however, Protestants and Catholics had learned to live side by
side as separate and distinct groups. Protestants, whose communicants included the king and queen, were in the majority, both in numbers and influence.

The new institution at Nijmegen sparked great enthusiasm among

Dutch Catholics. One of them, Titus, felt deeply honored when he was invited to join the university's first faculty as a professor of philosophy and mysticism.

His position at the university widened Titus' sphere of influence. His winning personality and genuine religious spirit attracted young people. His students gave him mixed reviews as a lecturer but highest grades as an approachable human being. He continued his writing apostolate and was eventually appointed superior of a monastery established near the university for students of the Carmelite Order.

From his quarters at Nijmegen, Titus—who spoke Italian, Frisian and English—was summoned constantly to hear confessions, give counsel and help the unfortunate. His apostolic spirit and his love for the Frisian people, who were mostly Protestant, drew him to establish a special Catholic society for Friesland. In 1926 he organized the first national pilgrimage to the site in Friesland where St. Boniface, who planted the faith in the region, was martyred in the eighth century. He continued work on various projects for his order. He also earned a reputation as a skillful lobbyist with the government on behalf of the university, and as a successful negotiator of government loans and grants for the institution.

In 1932 Titus was elected to a one-year term as rector magnificus, president, of the Catholic University of Nijmegen and accepted the office with joy and his customary deference.

Father Brandsma, at age 51, in the ceremonial robes as rector of the Catholic University of Nijmegen.

Titus proved to be an excellent administrator and rector. His non-threatening personality, his uncanny ability to reconcile hardheaded and opinionated university professors and administrators, and his negotiating skill all combined to make him truly a magnificent rector.

On the evening the university celebrated its 10th anniversary, the day after Titus' term as rector expired, students, alumni, and faculty members went to a local hotel for a celebration. Later that same evening, a group in high spirits left the hotel and paraded by torchlight to the Carmelite monastery. When Titus, responding to their enthusiastic demands for an immediate audience, appeared and tried to quiet the crowd, they accorded him a tumultuous ovation. The students and faculty he loved could hardly have paid him a more touching tribute.

*   *   *   *   *

After the expiration of his term as rector of the university, Titus returned to the classroom and lecture hall while continuing to commit himself to other apostolic endeavors which included writing and lecturing throughout the country. In 1935, at the request of his superiors in Rome, he undertook a lecture tour to Carmelite foundations in the United States, during which he traveled in the East and Midwest.

After a visit to Niagara Falls, he wrote in his journal:

> I am . . . contemplating the imposing Niagara Falls. From their high channel, I see them rushing down ceaselessly. . . . What is surprising is the marvelous and complex possibility of the waters. . . . I see God in the work of his hands and the marks of his love in every visible thing. I am seized by a supreme joy which is above all other joys.

Irish Carmelites who helped him perfect his use of English during a visit to their country before the United States tour, remembered him for his gentleness, humor and genuine goodness. They also marveled that Titus, unused to alcohol, consumed respectable amounts of potent Irish whiskey without showing any of the usual effects.

As the 1930s ended, Titus, despite nagging ill health, continued to mobilize every talent he possessed, every ounce of energy he could muster, to pursue his contemplative and active life.

In one of his lectures at Nijmegen, he revealed the source of his happiness and productivity:

> First of all, we have to see God as the fundamental basis for
> our being. This basis is hidden in the inner depth of our
> nature. There we have to see him and to meditate on him. . . .
> We then not only adore him in our own being but also in
> everything that exists.

Shortly before Titus left for the United States, Archbishop (later Cardinal) De Jong, ranking prelate of the Dutch hierarchy, appointed him spiritual advisor to the mostly lay staff members of the more than 30 Catholic newspapers in the country. The purpose of the appointment was to strengthen relations between the hierarchy and the working Catholic press. Titus, well-qualified for the liaison assignment, had no difficulty in winning the respect and cooperation of the journalists.

*   *   *   *   *

Adolf Hitler became Chancellor of Germany in January 1933. By that time he had already set in motion the forces of patriotism, political fanaticism, racial hatred and rigid party discipline that produced the Nazi dictatorship in Germany and prepared it for expansion into Austria, Czechoslovakia, the Scandinavian countries, Poland, Belgium, the Netherlands and France.

Titus, with sadness and foreboding, observed and correctly interpreted the ominous development of Nazism. In classroom, lecture hall and the press, he warned the Dutch against Hitler's tyranny. "The Nazi movement is a black lie," he proclaimed. "It is pagan." His critique and denunciation of the Nazi movement in Germany and its counterpart in Holland did not escape the notice of the Dutch National Socialist Party. He became a man marked for eventual reprisal.

German tanks bearing the swastika and flying red war banners burst across the Dutch frontier May 10, 1940, spearheading a blitzkrieg that rapidly crushed all organized military resistance.

With armed forces in command and Nazi officials and collaborators in political control, the repression of freedom became the objective in Holland. Accordingly, objectors to the occupation were deemed traitorous, organized religion came under attack, and Jews were victimized as they had already been in Germany.

Catholics came under strict regulation and straitened circumstances. Authorities decreed that priests and religious could not be principals or directors of secondary schools. The teaching salaries of priests and religious were cut by 40 percent. Catholic schools were ordered to expel Jewish students.

Appointed by the bishops, Titus appeared before officials at The Hague to present clearly and vigorously Catholic opposition to the crippling directives; to no avail.

The Dutch bishops announced January 26, 1941, that the sacraments were to be refused

> . . . to the Catholic of whom it was known that he was supporting the National-Socialist movement to a considerable extent . . . because it seriously endangers the Christian conception of life of all those who participate in it.

The bishops spoke again when the Nazis decreed a heavy-handed takeover of the Roman Catholic Workers' Union. In a letter addressed to the Dutch people in July 1941, they said:

> We have long maintained silence—that is to say, publicly—about the many injustices to which we Catholics have been submitted during recent months. . . .

The letter continued with a listing of injustices, stating in part:

> . . . We have been forbidden to hold collections . . . for our own charitable and cultural institutions. . . . Our Catholic broadcast . . . has been taken away from us. Our Catholic daily press has either been suspended or has been so limited in its freedom of expression that it is hardly possible any longer to speak of a Catholic Press. . . .

The letter also noted that some institutions had to pay exorbitant taxes and that youth groups had been forced to disband. The bishops then wrote:

> . . . Now something has happened about which we may no longer be silent without betraying our spiritual Office. . . . The Catholic Workers' Union is forced into the service of the National-Socialist movement; it becomes, in fact, one of its organizations. Therefore Catholics may no longer remain members.

That the bishops were forced to condemn Catholic membership in the union they had first established was a bitter pill for the church to swallow.

The bishops' letter goaded the military governor of the Netherlands to intensify persecution against both Jews and Catholics. Seyss-Inquart, an Austrian who had successfully engineered the annexation and incorporation of his own nation into the Third Reich, had spent the previous year trying to beguile the Dutch in the hope of turning them into willing collaborators with the Nazis. He failed to reckon upon one factor, however: the Dutch love of liberty. The people snickered at his blandishments.

After release of the bishops' letter, Seyss-Inquart declared open war on the Dutch in a speech delivered in August in Amsterdam:

> From this moment on it will be either you are with us or against us. The struggle will not be over until everyone accepts the way we, the Nazis, want things to be done. All of Europe will be chained and shackled before Germany gives up the fight. Nothing can prevent it.

The Nazi public relations bureau informed Dutch newspapers and journals that they had to accept advertisements and press releases emanating from official sources. Media personnel were told that "this measure which we have taken is based on the assumption that nothing may be omitted that may promote the unity of the Dutch nation."

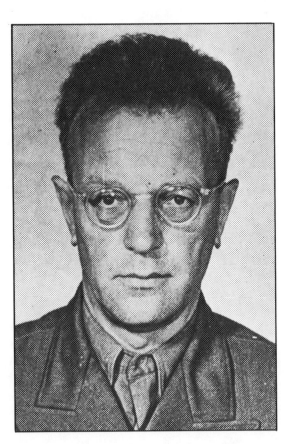

Nazi military governor Arthur Seyss-Inquart created a master plan for absorbing the Netherlands into the Third Reich.

Shortly after issuance of this memorandum, Archbishop De Jong summoned Titus to his chancery. "We will respond to them," he said. "Our answer must be 'No!' " He commissioned Titus, in his capacity as spiritual director of Catholic journalists, to convey the hierarchy's response personally to all Catholic editors in the Netherlands. On presenting this task the archbishop said: "Titus, you do understand this mission is dangerous. You do not have to undertake it."

The archbishop testified later,

Father Titus knew exactly what I said, and he freely and willingly accepted the duty. . . . The mission was necessary, for some of our editors disagreed with each other on what was allowed and in what cases they must disobey the new regulations because of their Catholic principles. Father Brandsma was the right man to explain our directives.

Titus wrote and began delivering to editors throughout the country a letter stating the bishops' directives and explaining the background. He encouraged the editors to resist Nazi demands while patiently explaining the various consequences of such resistance as well as of collaboration with occupation authorities. He concluded each visit with remarks along this line:

We have reached our limit. We cannot serve them. It will be our duty to refuse Nazi propaganda definitely if we wish to remain Catholic newspapers. Even if they threaten us with severe penalties, suspension or discontinuance of our newspapers, we cannot conform with their orders.

As he traveled from city to city, Titus was well aware that he was being shadowed by the Gestapo. Furthermore, someone informed the police of the purpose of his mission and the contents of his message.

Titus was a marked man.

*   *   *   *   *

Titus visited 14 editors before the Gestapo arrested him on Monday, January 19, 1942, at 6 p.m. at the Boxmeer monastery. He knelt and received the blessing of his superior. Leaving, he proudly wore in the lapel of his black clergy suit the insignia of a Knight of the Dutch Lion which he had received from Queen Wilhemina in August 1939. Police agents took him under guard to a prison at Scheveningen, a seaside port near The Hague. He was locked in cell 577.

"Imagine my going to jail at the age of 60," he said to his arresting officer.

"You should not have accepted the archbishop's commission," was the humorless reply.

Captain Hardegen, the tall, blond, always polite officer in charge of Titus' case, began his interrogation with the question: "Why have you disobeyed the regulations?"

"As a Catholic, I could have done nothing differently," Titus replied.

"You are a saboteur. Your church is trying to sabotage the orders of the occupying powers, to prevent the national socialistic philosophy of life from reaching the Dutch population."

Titus responded: "We must object to anything or any philosophy that is not in line with Catholic doctrine."

Three days later, Hardegen filed a report to Berlin in which he said:

> Brandsma's activity endangers the prestige of the German Empire, the national socialistic ideas, and intends to undermine the unity of the Dutch people. . . . It seems justifiable to take Professor Brandsma into custody for a considerable time.

But that was not all the Nazis had against the priest. Hardegen later explained that he was basically "an enemy of the German mission" and that "his hostility is proved by his writing against German policy toward the Jews."

As early as 1935, Titus had joined other Dutch intellectuals in public denunciation of Nazi persecution of the Jews.

Das Jahresbericht 1942 (the Nazis' "Yearbook 1942") summarized the occupiers' view of Titus and others like him. Under "News From Holland" it was reported that in that year 238 persons had been executed. The Secret Police had taken action against 10,000 Dutchmen. Following this item, the book gave details about the Nazi case against the church and, specifically, against the wicked Professor Brandsma:

Besides the publication of several episcopal letters and statements from the pulpit against socialism and against the N.S.B. (the Dutch Nazi Party), the Catholic clergy also tried to organize a big press campaign against the N.S.B., as well as against the "Arbeitsdienst" (voluntary labor for Germany) and the N.A.F. (the Socialist Labor Union). Through the arrest of Professor Brandsma (the leading man in this action)—this rebellion was quenched in its infancy.

*   *   *   *   *

In the evening of Wednesday, January 21, 1942, Captain Hardegen advised Titus that his case would require further hearings and that he would therefore be held at Scheveningen. He told him, "Life in your cell cannot be too difficult for you since you are a monk."

The officer allowed him to have his pipe and returned his watch. The hands were not set. "I have my own time," Titus wrote, "independent of Greenwich, Amsterdam or Berlin." During his years of intense apostolic activity, he had yearned for an opportunity to spend more time in prayer. The Nazis unwittingly gave him his heart's desire.

Titus, who had learned to love silence and solitude while a Frisian farm boy, had a genius for organization which soon found expression in a daily routine that was interrupted only when guards forced him out of it for interrogation sessions.

The interior of cell 577.

At one session Hardegen gave him a task: "Please advise me in writing, Professor Brandsma, why the Dutch people, particularly the Catholics, are objecting to the Dutch Nazi Party." Titus, candid and without fear, had no hesitation in spelling out why the Dutch would never accept the Nazis and why Hitler's dream of absorbing them into his empire was bound to fail.

He wrote:

> The Dutch have made great sacrifices out of love for God and possess an abiding faith in God whenever they have had to prove adherence to their religion. Protestants as well as Catholics venerate many martyrs from previous centuries who are examples for them. If it is necessary, we, the Dutch people, will give our lives for our religion. The Nazi movement is regarded by the Dutch people not only as an insult to God in relation to his creatures, but a violation of the glorious traditions of the Dutch nation. . . .

As Titus predicted, Nazi brutality succeeded in forging a bond between Protestants and Catholics in the Netherlands, a consequence the Nazis feared and an experience which the Dutch had not had since religious wars tore their churches apart centuries earlier.

Titus never hated the German people or individual members of the Nazi Party. At the end of his statement to Hardegen, he wrote:

> . . . God bless the Netherlands. God bless Germany. May God grant that both nations will soon be standing side by side in full peace and harmony.

Hardegen, declaring that "Brandsma feels he must protect Christianity against the National Socialists," regarded him as "very dangerous" and stated flatly: "We will not let him free before the end of the war."

Titus spent seven weeks in the uneasy silence that hung in the halls, corridors and salons of the resort turned into a prison at Scheveningen. Alone in his cell, he organized his day to the last moment. He wrote poetry, started a biography of St. Teresa of Avila, composed a series of meditations on the Way of the Cross for the Shrine of St. Boniface, martyr of Friesland, wrote two booklets (*My Cell, Letters From Prison*), read his breviary and knelt in silent prayer often during the day. He had a scheduled time for morning walks in the confines of his cell. He even smoked his pipe on

In cell 577 at the prison in Scheveningen, Titus wrote: "Though I am here alone, my Lord has never been closer to me. I even sing, though softly."

schedule—until January 29, the feast of St. Francis de Sales, patron of Catholic journalists, when guards peremptorily took away his pipe and tobacco. Imperturbable as always, he struck smoking time from his daily schedule.

"I felt at home in Scheveningen," he wrote to his Carmelite superior. "I pray, I write. The days are too short. I am very calm. I am happy and satisfied." So calm that he managed to complete six of 12 proposed chapters of his biography of St. Teresa.

* * * * *

On March 12 Titus was transported in a convoy with about 100 other prisoners—members of the underground, military personnel and clergy—to the notorious penal depot at Amersfoort.

On arrival there at about 9 p.m., guards marshalled the prisoners in the camp courtyard and ordered them to stand in freezing rain. Titus, clad in his black clerical suit, was a quiet figure of dignified defiance. After several hours in the rain the prisoners were led to a dressing room, ordered to strip, and handed prison uniforms. Then, before they could dress, they were driven naked out into the freezing rain. Finally the drenched and shivering men were herded into barracks and allowed to don the old army uniforms that were standard prison attire.

Titus, Number 58, was assigned to a work detail hacking out a shooting range in the forest surrounding Amersfoort. Prisoners, poorly equipped for the job of cutting trees, removing stumps and clearing ground, often dropped exhausted in their tracks. Disease, dysentery and despair were prevalent throughout the camp. When the hospital became overcrowded, guards laid the sick in the camp's muddy streets where late spring rains and cold nights brought merciful death to many. Others were taken on truck rides from which they never returned.

On April 20, Hitler's birthday, prison authorities granted amnesty to some fortunate prisoners. Titus was not among them. Through one of those released, however, he sent word to the Carmelites, telling them not to worry about him. "I will be all right," he assured them.

Released prisoners spoke of his good spirits, courage and generosity. "He frequently gives up a portion of his meager rations," they reported, "to help other starving prisoners."

"Particularly touching," one recalled, "is his care and concern for the Jews."

Guards strictly prohibited any priest or minister from giving spiritual counsel, and viciously punished violators. Jailers beat transgressors to death or left them maimed for life.

Titus quietly and coolly defied the ruling. On the days preceding Good Friday, he gathered groups of prisoners and led them through meditations on Christ's passion and the Stations of the Cross. Prisoners came to him every morning and night to ask for his blessing. He surreptitiously and silently made the Sign of the Cross on their hands with his thumb. He managed to hear confessions and even visited the sick and dying in the hospital.

Titus urged prisoners who could hardly bring themselves to forgive their brutal captors to "pray for them."

"Yes, Father," they replied, "but that is so difficult."

"You don't have to pray for them all day long," he counseled gently.

*   *   *   *   *

Nazi authorities celebrated Easter Sunday by sentencing 76 members of the Dutch underground to death. Other prisoners had to stand silently facing the condemned for over two hours. Titus prayed for them and signalled this to them whenever he could by folding his hands and pointing heavenward.

In late April the Gestapo ordered Titus from Amersfoort to Scheveningen for further interrogation. To all questions he repeated his original statement, that he acted out of principle and that, if he were again in the same circumstances, he would do exactly the same thing.

At the end of the questioning, Captain Hardegen informed him: "We have decided that you will be transferred to Dachau. You will stay there until the end of war."

En route to Dachau, Titus spent some time at a prison in Kleve, Germany, where he received relatively good treatment. He managed to assist at Mass and receive the Eucharist but was not permitted to offer the Holy Sacrifice.

Father Ludwig Deimel, the Catholic chaplain at Kleve, sought every opportunity to visit Titus. At his urging, Titus, whose health was deteriorating rapidly with the complication of uremic poisoning affecting his memory, appealed for parole. He asked to be allowed to spend his prison term at a Carmelite monastery in Germany.

His petition, unfortunately, was presented at the time Czechoslovakians assassinated Nazi Gauleiter Heydrich. Hardegen, who processed the petition, told Dutchmen who came to his office in support of the petition that security demanded Titus' continued imprisonment. "We are still on the battlefield, strong and unconquered," he lectured the Dutchmen, "and we intend to remain."

"In Dachau, I will meet friends, and God the Lord is everywhere," Titus wrote just before he left Kleve. "I could be in Dachau for a very long time. It doesn't have such a very good name that you really long for it."

On the journey from Kleve to Dachau the prisoners stopped briefly at a gigantic gymnasium in Nuremberg called The Turnhall. A prisoner described the place as "a vast reservoir of tears."

Dachau, one of Germany's oldest concentration camps, held over 110,000 prisoners from the time of its founding in the early 1930s. Eighty thousand prisoners died there.

From the very moment Titus entered the camp, his calmness and gentleness infuriated his captors. They beat him mercilessly with fists, clubs and boards. They kicked, punched and gouged him, drawing blood and oftentimes leaving him nearly unconscious in the mud.

The camp had a Catholic chapel where priests celebrated Mass every day. Prisoners were not allowed to attend, but intrepid inmates somehow were able to get and smuggle sacred hosts out to other prisoners.

One time Titus received the host in a tobacco pouch. Shortly after he got the pouch he was clubbed and kicked mercilessly by a guard who thought he had not mopped the kitchen floor. During the beating Titus kept one arm clenched tightly to his body. Finally he managed to crawl away from the enraged assailant and dragged himself to his bunk. A fellow Carmelite prisoner, Brother Tijhuis, came to comfort him., "Thank you, Brother," Titus said, "but don't have pity on me. I had Jesus with me in the Eucharist."

Three barracks in Dachau were reserved for about 1600 clergymen. "You will be in hell," a Dachau veteran told Titus when he was assigned to one of the barracks. "There," the prisoner added, "men die like rats." Of 2000 Polish priests imprisoned there, 850 died before the war's end.

The prisoners' day began at 4 a.m. All day long guards chased them, exacted extra hours of labor, cut their miserable rations, harassed, hounded, beat and bludgeoned them. Work began at 5:30 a.m. and continued until 7 p.m., with a lunch break.

Titus, already suffering from untreated uremic poisoning, contracted a severe foot infection. The open sandals which prisoners wore caused his feet to blister and eventually suppurate. At the end of the workday, fellow

In 1952 a committee was formed to begin the process of beatification for
Father Brandsma.

prisoners often carried him to the barracks. Father Urbanski, a Polish
prisoner, who more than once carried him, remembered:

> So even-tempered and approachable was he, so cheerful in
> the midst of disaster which was threatening us from all sides,
> that he deeply touched our hearts.

Another prisoner recalled that "he radiated with cheerful courage."

Titus continuously exhorted his fellow prisoners: "Do not yield to
hatred. Be patient. We are here in a dark tunnel but we have to go on. At the
end, the eternal light is shining for us."

In his very last letter home, Titus, broken in body, full of infection,
bruised, and with hardly a sound spot within or without, wrote:

With me, everything is fine. You have to get used to new situations. With God's help, this is working out all right. Don't worry too much about me. In Christ. Your Anno.

*   *   *   *   *

Titus, although he knew his days were numbered, refused to enter Dachau's hospital. He knew that in that hellish place inhumanity plumbed new depths. Doctors used prisoners for medical experimentation. Many human guinea pigs suffered frightfully before dying indescribable deaths. The few survivors were ruined for life.

Finally Titus had no choice. He entered the hospital in the early part of the third week of July. He too became a subject for medical experimentation. In the afternoon of Sunday, July 26, 1942, the doctor in charge of his case ordered him injected with a deadly drug. Within 10 minutes Father Titus Brandsma, who brought happiness wherever he went on this earth—even to Dachau—was dead.

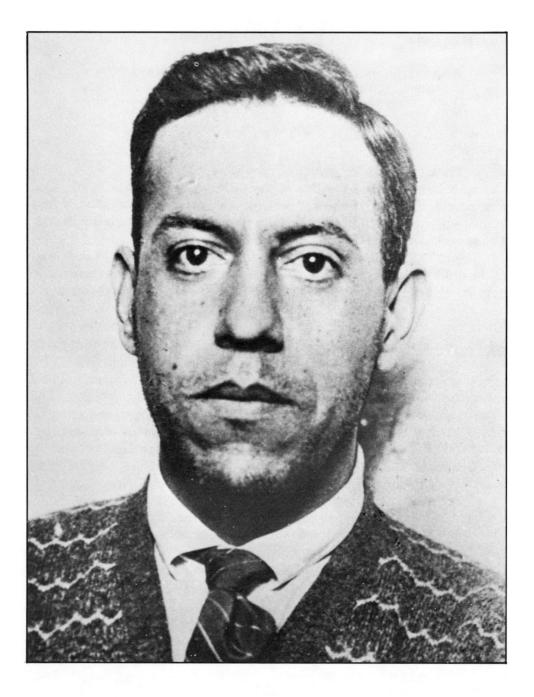

Miguel Pro

"Oh, Miguel, you're awful! How could you embarrass me so in front of all those people?" Senorita Maria de la Concepcion Pro's complaint, hurled over her shoulder as she strode away from her 16-year-old brother, doubled the tormentor over with laughter. His mirth only further infuriated his older sister. She wheeled about, her dark eyes flashing with anger, and stared at him. Suddenly she too burst into laughter, more at him than anything else.

"Oh, Miguel, I'll never trust you again!" The 18-year-old girl and her mischievous brother stopped dead in their tracks on the dusty Mexican road and continued laughing heartily at each other.

The reason for their gaiety was an incident that had occurred only moments before. The two, walking along a back road high in the mountains of central Mexico, had encountered a roadside auction. The auctioneer, clever and glib, presented and rapidly sold a series of articles and animals to some of the people gathered before him. Suddenly he led a flea-bitten, rheumy-eyed burro to the auction block. The beast featured a lackluster coat, an evident limp and one slightly chewed ear. The auctioneer, despite a powerful sales pitch and clever quips, was able to stir little interest in the burro. "One-half peso," a brave soul ventured. The abysmally low bid hung in the hot afternoon air. The auctioneer, sweating beneath the sun, begged and pleaded with his uninterested audience. No amount of verbal wizardry could disguise the animal's evident age and infirmities.

The vendor continued his hard sell. "Not since holy Joseph purchased a burro to bring the holy Virgin and Christ Child back from Egypt has so fine a beast been presented for sale," he wheedled. Even this appeal to the Mexican love for the holy family elicited no response.

Suddenly Concepcion cried out, or so it seemed, "Two and one-half pesos."

The auctioneer, hardly believing his ears, pounded his gavel and quickly brought the sale to closure. "And now, young lady, this magnificent burro is yours."

"But, Senor, I did not make a bid on this beautiful creature!"

"Senorita, with all due respect, you did, and all these ladies and gentlemen heard your very words. Now you must pay and take this fine burro as your very own."

"But, Senor, I do not have any money!"

"What a sadness that is, Senorita."

"I am sorry," the girl apologized, "but I did not bid, Senor. I never opened my mouth."

"Who did then, if you did not?" the disappointed auctioneer inquired.

"Senor, I cannot tell you the one who bid. Of only one thing am I sure, that he is a person who is no longer here. Also of one other thing I am sure, that I do not have even one peso, even one-half peso, to purchase this poor burro."

Concepcion spoke the truth on both scores. She had no money and Miguel, who had mimicked her expertly, was hiding behind a nearby shed and quaking with repressed laughter.

Her brother had once more executed a practical joke on poor Concepcion. He knew his sister would be angry with him, but not for long. No one could remain angry for long with Miguel Pro.

*   *   *   *   *

Good fortune had smiled on Miguel Agustin Pro Juarez since his birth on January 13, 1891, in Guadalupe, central Mexico. His father,

Miguel Pro

Miguel, a mining engineer, was both wealthy and kind. His mother, Josefa Juarez, was a woman of wisdom and charity. Her first two children, Maria de la Concepcion and Maria de la Luz, helped her raise Miguel. She needed all the help she could get with her lively son. He was born to mischief. He teased his sisters, played endless pranks on the family and servants, and even ran up unauthorized bills at the candy store. More than once his father bent Miguel over his knee to implant wisdom on the boy's backside. In his judgment, Miguel was a slow learner—at least of wisdom.

Young Miguel reveled in the free, wild land of Mexico's silver-mining region where the family made their home. The magnificent pine-covered mountains and the luminous white clouds that sailed slowly across the vast blue skies fascinated the boy. He would drag poor Concepcion along on one mountain climb after another. "Let's get to the top, Concepcion," he would plead, "that way we can see more sky." Often the two of them would tumble into the dark ravines and return home cut and bruised.

The young Pro was a robust boy even after a bout with poisoning that was complicated by measles.

Once when Miguel unwittingly ate toxic berries, poison spread throughout his system and brought on a high fever. His limbs stiffened, his head lolled about, and he lost the power of speech. The usually lively boy fell into a torpor that continued for an entire year. While in this condition, he contracted measles. Doctors prepared his parents for the worst.

After hearing the medical report, Miguel's father, who had often bent the little one over his knee, took his son in his arms and, kneeling before a statue of Our Lady of Guadalupe, lifted him up to Mary. "O Mother Mary," he prayed, "give me back my child!" The little body trembled, and the boy expelled a clot of blood from his mouth. The fever soon subsided, light came back into the roguish black eyes, speech returned—and Miguel was soon teasing his sisters and brothers again.

The Pro children received their early education at home, first from their father and then from private tutors. When Miguel was 10, he went to Mexico City to attend a Catholic school. Unfortunately, a severe stomach ailment, from which he suffered the rest of his life, forced him to return home. He then attended a non-sectarian boarding school in Saltillo near his father's silver mines in Concepcion del Oro. The anti-Catholic principal there forbade him to assist at Mass. The man would not let him leave school on Sundays and even intercepted his letters of complaint to his father. Through friends, Miguel finally contacted home. His father hastened to Saltillo to remove him from the school.

After these two unhappy experiences at boarding school, Miguel's father kept him at home and arranged for him to continue his studies under private tutors.

In 1905 Miguel's father settled the family for a short period of time in a beautiful home in Saltillo. He remained at the mining site he managed in Concepcion del Oro during the week and returned home to spend weekends with his wife and seven children. Four Pro children had died in infancy or childhood. Miguel, the oldest son, exerted his natural leadership over all the children. He organized his brothers and sisters into a theatrical company that performed evening musicals for their parents and the servants. Inevitably he, a guitarist, starred in the shows. He already evidenced a genuine talent for music, acting, mimicry and mime. His mobile face could simultaneously be doleful on one side and uproariously comical on the other.

Miguel Pro, standing at center, and his family. His father was driven into hiding by the anti-Catholic Mexican government; his mother Josefa suffered from poverty and illness.

At the age of 15 Miguel joined the office staff at his father's mines in Concepcion del Oro. The boy acquitted himself well at his first employment. A skilled draftsman and excellent bookkeeper, he was also an expert typist.

Although content and capable, Miguel knew that desk work would never suit him. Because he needed contact with people, he spent his free time at the mine shaft chatting with the miners. His talent for mimicry enabled him to learn their special vocabulary and manners of speech. Even though he was the boss's son, workers felt comfortable with him. The hard-bitten laborers sensed the youth's respect for them. Often when a shift of miners surfaced after long hours underground, they would find him waiting to entertain them with an impromptu comic and musical performance.

He did more than entertain the miners. While still a child, he often accompanied his mother on her visits to sick and needy miners and their families. Josefa nursed the ill and provided food and clothing for the needy. Soon after Miguel began working in his father's office, the Pro family promoted and established a hospital for workers, an uncommon act of mercy in a land where the rich ruthlessly exploited the poor.

*   *   *   *   *

Miguel, in love at 17, courted a beautiful young lady. The girl, a Protestant, admired many things about Miguel—his buoyant spirit, his Latin energy and flair, his marvelous and magical mimicry—but found it difficult to accept his Catholicism, and especially his deep, persistent devotion to the Blessed Mother. The two broke off the relationship, much to the relief of Josefa who felt God was calling her son to the priesthood.

Josefa kept these thoughts to herself. She refused to exert any pressure on Miguel, knowing well that he was obstinate enough to respond negatively to any of her efforts to decide his life's work.

He did not think seriously of his future career until his older sisters, Luz and Concepcion, entered the cloistered Good Shepherd Sisters at Aguascalientes. Miguel, unable to accept the separation, especially from Concepcion, was angry and depressed; more than once he broke into tears. "*Caramba*," he groaned one evening, "heaven must be a wonderful place if it is bought at such a price."

"Go and make a retreat, Miguel," counseled his mother. "Maybe God will help you understand why the girls left our home." He went, but only to please his mother. He returned home in good spirits and at peace with God and himself. He had also decided his life's work. "I am going to join the Jesuits," he told his parents.

In the summer of 1911 the Jesuits accepted Miguel Pro as a candidate for their Society and ordered him to their novitiate in Michoacan to begin the 14 years of training required for priesthood in the Society of Jesus.

Father Santiago, the novice master, quickly and accurately sized up Miguel. The boy blended in his character a mixture of seriousness and gaiety that augured well for his future as a priest. Sometimes he would catch the novice master completely off guard. "Father, I want to go back home to Concepcion del Oro," he told Father Santiago one day.

His first few years in the seminary were peaceful, but as the church-state struggle intensified, the seminarians were forced to flee to other countries to study. Miguel is at the bottom right.

"Why?" the master asked.

"Because before I came here I was very fond of the Jesuits, but now I just can't stand them, not even Your Reverence."

The novice master was magnanimous enough to laugh at such injudicious remarks.

A fellow novice remembered Miguel as an ideal companion at recreation time and a principal actor in sessions organized on certain feast days. However, one could easily discern in him two sides: He was the life of the party during recreation time, and a religious man of profound interior life.

On August 15, 1913, Miguel professed his first vows.

*   *   *   *   *

A few years before Miguel entered the Jesuit novitiate, Mexico convulsed into violent and vicious civil war.

From the time the nation achieved its independence from Spain in 1821, it had experienced a calamitous series of civil and religious wars, foreign invasions and counterrevolutions. Endless conflicts exhausted its energies and resources. In 1848 the United States invaded the country and defeated its proud armies. The United States seized one-half of Mexico's territories as the prize of war.

At the time of Miguel's birth Mexico enjoyed some measure of peace and tranquility because Dictator Porfirio Diaz ruled the country with an iron hand. The wily Diaz managed to maintain a shaky balance among Mexico's three great power blocs—the wealthy landowners, the Catholic church and the army. But after a "presidency" of 31 years he was driven from office by revolutionaries in 1911. Hardly had the rebels seized power before they fell in violent frenzy on each other. For two decades rival armies roamed the land, pillaging, burning, raping. Fighting was savage. No quarter was asked and none was given. Mass executions of men and women frequently followed military defeat. Firing squads were common sights. A man who personally killed hundreds once suffered a blister on his trigger finger from executing one by one a corral full of prisoners. Soldiers wounded in combat had little medical assistance and frequently died from infections of their wounds. Between 1910 and 1920, Mexico's bloodiest decade, the nation's population diminished by one million people.

The Pro family had survived these perilous times relatively unscathed. Inexorably, however, the tragic wave of terror flowed toward them.

General Venustiano Carranza, after uniting all revolutionary forces under his leadership in 1913, vowed to restore order to the land. Although personally moderate in his relations with the church, he could not restrain his henchmen who were determined to break the church's power and seize its wealth. Cruel and vicious revolutionaries drove priests from their rectories, defiled tabernacles and sanctuaries, and brutally persecuted Catholics who opposed the revolution. Miguel's father, a loyal Catholic, was forced under threat of death to leave his wife and family in Guadalajara and go into hiding. Revolutionaries seized all his property.

Miguel, heartbroken and powerless to help, heard the news of his family while he was a novice.

The Jesuits were favorite whipping boys of the revolutionaries. On August 15, 1913, troops broke into the novitiate, forcing the community at Michoacan to disperse and go underground. Dressed as laymen, the Jesuits made their way in small groups to the American frontier and freedom. They reorganized at the American Jesuit novitiate in Los Gatos, California, where they remained for the next year and a half. Miguel, always a quick study, learned to speak English there.

Since most of the Mexican students felt more at home in the Hispanic culture, Jesuit authorities sent the band of exiles to the Society's house of studies in Granada, Spain.

From the fall of 1915 until the summer of 1920, Miguel continued his studies in Spain.

Despite the sufferings of exile, the debilitation of his physical health, his worries about his parents and family in their troubled homeland, his spirits remained buoyant and his sense of humor intact. "One day," a superior recalled, "I called attention to the fact that his jokes sometimes went too far and might reflect on the level of education in Mexico."

Miguel swiftly replied, "Oh, Father, my jokes are not the Mexican type; they are the Pro type."

Miguel discovered that his confreres at Granada were as receptive to his entertainment as the silver miners of Concepcion del Oro. "We used to hurry to wherever he was assigned to manual labor," a fellow Jesuit remembered, "because, before he would start work, he would go into his antics—which put all of us in the best of humor." Only a few of his fellow religious knew that he suffered constant pain from his stomach disorder. Worsening news from Mexico aggravated the condition.

"I know," the rector at Granada recalled, "that the bad news he received from home often broke his heart but never disturbed the serenity of his soul. He bore his trials with admirable patience and was always ready to console and cheer others who were bearing sufferings of their own."

*   *   *   *   *

In Miguel's time the Jesuit training program scheduled a two- or three-year pause between philosophical and theological studies. At this stage candidates for the priesthood, called scholastics, generally taught school. Miguel, after completing his studies in philosophy, joined the staff of a boarding school run by the Jesuits in Nicaragua. His health suffered in the hot, damp Nicaraguan climate and his spirits drooped ever so slightly. "I'm not going through such a happy time here," he wrote to a fellow Jesuit. Despite his lack of enthusiasm for Nicaraguan boarding school life, however, he did not lose his sense of humor or sensitivity to his students or fellow religious. He remained a willing and cheerful co-worker. He was nonetheless delighted to return to Spain for the start of theological studies in September 1922.

Two years later Father Crivelli, supervisor of the Mexican Jesuits' training, sent Miguel to the house of studies at Enghein, Belgium, to pursue social studies. Crivelli reported to the superior general:

After his philosophy studies, Miguel taught at a boys' boarding school in Nicaragua.

Pro does not shine as regards his studies; but among all our students he stands out for his common sense. We need in this field men who can thoroughly understand the laboring man's mentality; priests who are cheerful and who attract the workers.

The field Father Crivelli wrote about was the apostolate of Catholic social action. Pope Leo XIII issued a landmark encyclical, *Rerum Novarum,* on the subject in May 1891, for the purpose of mobilizing the Roman Catholic world's intellectual, moral and spiritual forces to provide Christian solutions to the social ills of modern man. He challenged the church to abandon the defensive posture it had assumed since the Reformation and to initiate an aggressive campaign to rescue the world's working people from godless solutions to their ever-worsening plight.

"We are losing the working classes from the church," the pope warned. "We must take bold initiative on their behalf."

Leo summoned every priest and religious "to bring to the struggle the full energy of his mind and all his powers of endurance." Miguel's assignment in Belgium was part of the Jesuit response to the pope's challenge to religious orders.

The significance of Leo's encyclical dawned on the Mexican church slowly. But as early as 1903 Mexican Catholics, lay and clerical, inaugurated a series of national congresses dedicated to themes of social justice. Catholic worker organizations of men and women came into being. By 1911 Catholics organized a political arm called the National Catholic Party. Male and female college students bound together in various youth movements became enthusiastic auxiliaries to the political arm.

Mexican revolutionaries viewed this Catholic mobilization with suspicion. Children of the atheistic French Revolution, the anticlerical revolutionaries sought to obliterate all traces of Christianity from the nation's culture. "Social ills," they proclaimed, "come from adhering to outmoded social structures, especially the church which denies the basic rights of men and oppresses the poor." Mexico's rulers viewed the church as an enemy of social progress and held the clergy responsible for much of the evil that was destroying the nation.

In 1917 Venustiano Carranza issued a new constitution that put every facet of church life under government control. Seminaries were closed, monasteries of men and women religious were shut down, the number of priests in each area of the country was controlled by government decree. The constitution resolved once and for all the struggle between church and state; it simply ceased to recognize the church as a legal institution in the nation.

The young Catholic elite refused to be bullied by the tyrants. Rarely did they shrink from a fight. Organizing demonstrations, protests, riots and boycotts, they resisted the government at every turn.

Heriberto Navarrete aptly described the spirit that animated these young heroes:

> We learned, little by little, that man's life on earth is a fierce battle and those who live it best are those who are the most warlike, who master themselves and then throw themselves against the army of evil to conquer by dying, and leave to their children the inestimable legacy of heroic example.

Anacleto Gonzalez Flores, a lawyer and respected lay leader, clarified in four words the commitment of young Catholic Mexicans to Christian social progress: "It is unto death."

*   *   *   *   *

In Belgium, far from Mexico's turbulence, Miguel pressed on with his studies, hoping that his superiors would not deny him priestly orders because of his poor physical condition. His fears proved unfounded. On August 30, 1925, the 34-year-old exile received the sacrament of holy orders. "I could not keep back the tears," he wrote to a confrere, "when I first pronounced with the bishop the words of consecration."

Unlike the other Jesuits ordained that day, Miguel had no member of his family on whom he could bestow his first priestly blessing. "I went to my room," he recalled, "laid out all the photographs of my family on the table, and then blessed each one from the bottom of my heart."

During the year following ordination Miguel's severe stomach ailment persisted. Doctors operated three times without affording him any relief from pain.

In February 1926, while in the hospital recuperating from a second operation and preparing for a third, he received a telegram from Mexico informing him of his mother's death. "The blow was hard," he remembered. "My dream of returning to Mexico to give holy communion to my dear mother has faded away. All the evening after I received the telegram I was quite stunned. During the night, crucifix in hand, I wept a great deal."

In June 1926 Miguel sailed for Mexico and disembarked July 7 at Vera Cruz. He reported immediately to his superiors in Mexico City.

Three weeks later revolutionary President Plutarco Elias Calles proclaimed his intention to completely enforce all anti-Catholic provisions of the infamous Constitution of 1917. He determined to achieve a final solution to Mexico's church and state problem.

The Mexican bishops, as obstinate and defiant as their enemies, called a priests' strike for Sunday, August 1, 1926; their purpose was to provoke public wrath against the government. For the first time in over 400 years no priest entered a Mexican sanctuary to celebrate Mass. Instead, priests emptied the tabernacles, concealed the sacred vessels and snuffed out the sanctuary lamps. The tough Mexican bishops ordered the church underground.

Miguel, assigned to Mexico City, was in the vortex of the anticlerical tornado. "I go around every day to distribute holy communion to about 300 people at places I call my eucharistic stations," he told a friend. "To baffle government agents who go around here like night birds, I change my route each day."

Miguel with his two brothers.

He fully realized the danger of his mission and sensed that someday he would pay a fierce price for his priestly vocation. He wrote to a friend:

> Reprisals are merciless, above all in Mexico City. If only I could be among the number who must shed their blood. If it happens, prepare your petitions for heaven because I will only be too happy to present them there.

Calles, again and again proclaiming his intention to obliterate Catholicism, did not hesitate to beat, maul and murder Catholics who opposed him. An extraordinarily cruel man, he once hung a peasant with barbed wire for verbally criticizing him.

Early in the strike revolutionaries executed 20 members of the Catholic youth organizations. "The list of martyrs," Miguel wrote, "grows longer every day."

He organized his own underground so well that he seemed to be everywhere at once. On the first Friday of November 1926, he administered the Eucharist to 1300 people. He heard confessions, celebrated Mass, anointed the sick, blessed marriages, baptized babies and cared for the poor.

Miguel's superiors, fearful for his life, ordered him to a hiding place. Furious because of his removal from the arena of pastoral ministry, he nevertheless obeyed. From his hiding place he kept up a steady barrage of pleas to his superiors to reassign him to the underground:

> My life, what does it matter? Of course, one must not throw one's life away stupidly. But, what kind of followers of St. Ignatius are we if, after having entered the battle, we run after the first shot is fired?

He added a curious postscript:

> My health is vastly improved. My stomach hardly remembers its operations. It flutters like angels' wings from time to time simply to remind me that it is there. Only this gentle reminder after years of daily attacks and three operations!

His superiors finally relented, and Miguel hurried back to his catacombs. He initiated a series of underground retreats. He assumed the dress of whatever group he led in retreat and cheerfully administered the sacraments and word of God to them. "I gave the taxi drivers their retreat in an open-air garage dressed as a mechanic," he wrote. "Strike me pink, I could speak their language from my days at the mines!"

To sacramental ministry he joined immense works of charity. He found the poor everywhere and raised money to provide shelter, clothing and food for them. He was particularly solicitous for families whose members suffered death, imprisonment or exile during the persecution. At one time, although without fixed resources, he supported no less than 100 families.

One day a nun, noticing that he was feverish, reminded him that he had not eaten during the previous 24 hours.

"Eat? Maybe I did, maybe I didn't," he responded. "Who knows?" Once more his characteristic humor flashed like a fencer's foil. "You see, Sister, I went to a dentist yesterday and the barbarian broke my jawbone, or if you prefer, my mandible. How can one dine without a proper mandible?"

*   *   *   *   *

Calles put a price on Miguel's head in January 1927. Many police officers and citizens were anxious to collect the bounty. But Miguel, the mimic and actor, proved difficult to run to earth. "He is," someone noted, "everywhere and nowhere." He learned how to shake a police tail, quickly change his clothes, rearrange his hair, manipulate his cigarette, change the expression on his face and distract the attention of people seeking to identify him.

Miguel, running on one occasion from a police trap, turned a corner and found himself in a blind alley. Trapped, he thought. Just then a young woman whom he knew passed the alley. A devilish wink set up the charade. The police running into the alley saw no fugitive priest—only a couple apparently very much in love strolling past them.

In the coveralls and hat of a worker he conducted retreats underground.

Another time, he arrived near a house where people had gathered for a clandestine Mass. Two policemen guarded the door. "If I turn away, the police will suspect me," he thought. "If I go in, I'll get caught and will compromise everybody waiting inside." Later, he described how he resolved the dilemma:

> I walked straight up to the cops with an air of being in on the secret. I jotted down the number of the house, drew back my lapel as if to show them my detective's badge and commented darkly, "There's an eel here under the rock!" The two cops threw me a superb military salute and swept open the door for me to enter.

He described another amusing incident:

> In spite of strict secret police surveillance [Mexico had more than 10,000 agents at that time], I can baptize, marry, and take Viaticum to the dying. I have even come

Ministering to an underground
church required many disguises.
Here he is pictured in street clothes.

across the dying in places where I have been called for other duties. Once, at six o'clock in the morning, I was halfway through the Communion of the Mass when a maid rushed in crying: "The police are here!" The people assisting at the Mass were terrified. "Keep calm," I counseled them. "Conceal your religious emblems and disperse into the different rooms of the house. Above all, no noise." I was wearing that day a cap and a light gray suit that from long usage verged on dark gray. I took out a cigarette and inserted it in an enormously long holder. Then I hid the Blessed Sacrament on my breast and received the intruders.

"There is public worship going on here," the police said to me.

"There is not," I replied.

"Yes, yes, there is public worship here," the police insisted.

"Well, this time you have been fooled," I growled.

"How fooled? We saw a priest come in here. And anyhow we have orders to visit and search the premises. Follow us!"

"I like that! This is the last straw! Follow you? And by what right can you try and make me? Show me your search warrant. However, if you are bent on it, go all over the house and, if you find public worship going on, come and tell me so that I can hear Mass."

The clever Miguel helped the police search for the priest, whom they never found. At the end of the episode the police stood outside the door, guarding it lest a priest enter. Meanwhile, inside, Father Pro resumed distributing communion to the faithful.

* * * * *

Father Miguel Pro looked deeply into the sombre night that had fallen on his beloved country. He discerned in all of the horror the face of the crucified Christ. With all his heart he yearned to join his sufferings with the Mexican church as it drank deeply its bitter chalice of pain. "Pray to God that I am granted the grace to die a martyr," he requested of a fellow priest. On Sunday, November 13, 1927, he wrote a prayer to the Blessed Mother in which he offered to stand beneath the cross of Christ with her.

Allow me to spend my life near to thee, O my Mother! Let me accompany you in your sorrow and loneliness. . . . What I really want in my life is the mocking and sneering of Mount Calvary. I desire that slow agony of thy Son; the contempt, the ignominy and the infamy of the cross. What I desire, O most sorrowful Virgin, is to stand close to you, so as to fortify my spirit by your tears, consummate my sacrifice by your martyrdom, sustain my heart by your solitude, and love my God and your God by the immolation of my whole being.

*   *   *   *   *

A number of Catholic youth groups became increasingly militant as Calles' persecutions continued. One group, known as the Cristeros, mounted armed resistance to the revolution. The hierarchy and the Holy See viewed them with mixed feelings. The youths had every right to oppose the revolution and resist their oppressors, but church authorities could not countenance their resorting to violence.

The Cristeros considered themselves crusaders willing to lay down their lives to restore Christ to Mexican life. Their morale was superb; their courage in combat, fearsome. At the consecration of the Mass they stood at attention, presented their weapons to Christ and filled the air with cries of, *"Viva Cristo Rey"* ("Long Live Christ the King"). By 1927 ten thousand of them were engaged in guerrilla warfare against federal troops. Although ill-equipped, they acquitted themselves well in combat with the well-trained federal forces.

Two of Miguel's brothers, Humberto and Roberto, were active in other Catholic youth groups although they did not belong to the Cristeros, and they got Miguel involved in their work. He was in charge of a project financed by Catholic youth which was designed to care for the widows and orphans of Cristeros who died in combat. He did not hesitate to give spiritual and material help to those who were smuggling supplies to the rebels.

On November 13, 1927, a Cristero leader led an assassination attack on Alvaro Obregon, a revolutionary general destined to succeed Calles as Mexico's next president. The squad poured a hail of bullets and threw bombs at Obregon's car as it passed through the streets of Mexico City that quiet

Sunday afternoon. After the attack, which Obregon miraculously survived, the assassins fled the scene in their car, an Essex. Police followed them in a wild chase through the city. The pursuit ended when the Essex collided with another vehicle. Police arrested two assailants, Juan Tirado and Nahum Ruiz. Ruiz, struck by a police bullet, died soon after capture. Tirado was thrown in jail. Two other men escaped into the crowd.

Police investigators traced the registration of the Essex. Its owner was Humberto Pro.

Meanwhile Obregon, only slightly wounded, returned home, washed, changed his clothes and went to the bullfights. A few moments after he arrived at the arena, Segura Vilchis, the architect of the assassination plot, purchased tickets to the bullfight and sat in a box near Obregon. The tickets were his alibi for the afternoon of Sunday, November 13, 1927.

Police authorities, convinced that the Pro brothers were involved in the attack, arrested Humberto and Roberto. A police agent squeezed from a young boy the whereabouts of Father Miguel and arrested him.

When Vilchis heard that the three brothers had been arrested, he immediately went to police headquarters and confessed the crime. He insisted that they were completely innocent, but his words made little difference for Humberto and Miguel, who were condemned to die before a firing squad; Roberto was set free in due course. On the morning of November 23, 1927, Juan Tirado, Segura Vilchis, Humberto and Father

Pro's relentless activity finally led to his execution. Here he prays before facing the firing squad.

Miguel Pro went one by one before the firing squad. Calles ordered photographs taken of the executions for public display.

In the manner of all brave Mexicans, Father Pro refused the blindfold and stood calmly before his executioners. He extended his arms in the form of a cross. "With all my heart I forgive my enemies," he said aloud. Just before the order to fire was given, he softly pronounced the words that so clearly expressed the meaning of his life and all his works: *"Viva Cristo Rey."*

The following day thousands of people attended funeral services for the brothers in Mexico City. Scornful of secret agents, ten thousand Mexicans lined the route of the procession, waving palms and throwing flowers. "There was nothing mournful about that funeral," a Jesuit remembered. "Cheering and singing filled the air." As the caskets passed through the streets the crowds cried out: *"Viva Cristo Rey."*

At the grave site, Senor Pro knelt alone beside Miguel's and Humberto's caskets. After a short prayer he rose and, with head held high, walked back to where the rest of the family were standing. "It is, my children, the end," he said, and then added *"Te Deum Laudamus"* ("We praise you, O

Anna Maria Pro claimed the bodies of her brothers, Miguel and Humberto, and held the wake at her home. Their father stands near the center facing a casket.

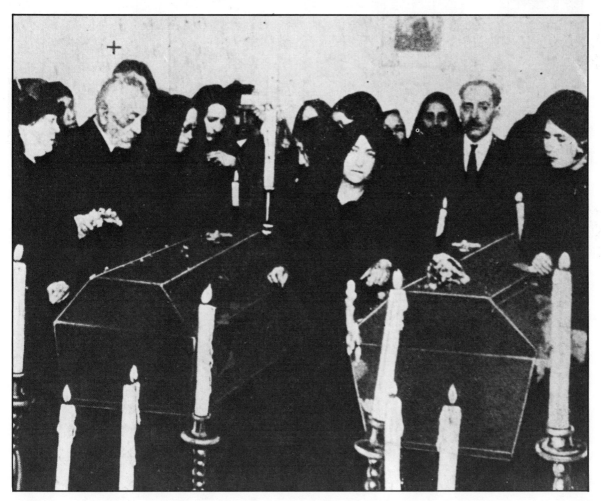

Thousands jammed the funeral of the Pro brothers: an outpouring that
paid tribute to their faith and courage.

God"). The people around the grave took up the words, *"Te Deum
Laudamus,"* and gave triumphant voice to the church's traditional hymn of
praise and thanksgiving.

Father Miguel Pro of the Society of Jesus had witnessed with his
blood to Christ, his king.